EAT DRINK
MAN WOMAN

THE
WEDDING
BANQUET

EAT DRINK MAN WOMAN

THE WEDDING BANQUET

TWO FILMS BY

ANG LEE

THE OVERLOOK PRESS

WOODSTOCK • NEW YORK

First published in 1994 by
The Overlook Press
Lewis Hollow Road
Woodstock, New York 12498

Library of Congress Cataloging-in-Publication Data

Two films by Ang Lee / introduction by James Schamus.
p. cm.
Contents: Eat Drink Man Woman / Hui Ling Wang, Ang Lee, James Schamus–
The Wedding Banquet / Neil Peng, Ang Lee, James Schamus.
1. Motion picture plays. I. Lee, Ang. II. Schamus, James.
III. Wang, Hui-Ling, 1964- Eat Drink Man Woman. 1994.
IV. Peng, Neil. The Wedding Banquet. 1994.
PN1997.A1T86 1994
791.45'75–dc20
94-27236
CIP
ISBN: 0-87951-568-6
First Edition

CONTENTS

INTRODUCTION
James Schamus

T HE two scripts printed here represent the two poles of director Ang Lee's current existence—New York and Taipei—as well as the two underlying currents that inform his art—American narrative cinema and Chinese philosophy. A native of Taiwan, who came to the states a decade ago to study theater at the University of Illinois, Ang has perfectly acclimated to America even as he has refused to assimilate. By maintaining his creative distance from American culture while mastering its most dominant expression of itself, Ang has managed to create a uniquely individual cinema that can speak to people everywhere.

Ang came to the cinema through his theater studies, and ended up at New York University film school in the early eighties, where he made a forty-minute graduate film, *Fine Line*, that caught the attention of Hollywood and landed him an agent and a string of development deals. Ang spent the next six years writing scripts, cooking dinner for his wife and two sons, and waiting for his big break. It never came. But he did win a screenwriting competition back in Taipei, and made the acquaintance of Li-Kong Hsu, the former director of Taiwan's cinematheque and now the vice president of Taiwan's biggest film production company, Central Motion Picture Corporation.

Hsu was willing to gamble on Ang, but the only problem was that Ang's script, *Pushing Hands*, took place not in Taipei but in New York. It told the story of a retired Tai Chi master, who moves to the States from Beijing to live with his son—who is married with child to an American woman. The resulting domestic culture clash leads to a string of debacles, with Grandpa eventually running away to China-town to work as an exploited dishwasher, only to have his Tai Chi skills turn him into an overnight hero.

With only $450,000 to spend on the film—a fine budget by Taiwanese standards at the time, but barely the cost of a one-minute MacDonald's ad in the states—Ang was in a bind that, luckily, my partner, Ted Hope, and I were able to solve. Ted had been a huge fan of Ang's NYU student film, but when we formed our production company, Good Machine, we thought that Ang's busy Hollywood schedule meant that he was untouchable for low-budget types like us. We had cut our teeth working in various producing roles for a number of American independents—Ted most notably for Hal Hart-ley on films like *Trust* and *Simple Men*, I for producer Christine Vachon on films like *Poison* and *Swoon*—and we were known as specialists at "no-budget" production.

But, of course, Ang had no interest in no-budget production, and our first working collaboration, on *Pushing Hands*, in the summer of 1991, was an all-out commercial feature film, with hundreds of extras, fight choreography, and a cast of Taiwanese stars. Somehow, with the help of a dedicated Chinese-American community in New York and an equally dedicated crew, Ang brought it in on budget, and the film went on to be a hit in Asia. And so we were presented with the chance to make *The Wedding Banquet*—this time with the enormous sum of $750,000.

The story of *The Wedding Banquet's* eventual success has already become industry legend: *Variety*, for example, in its list of the most profitable films of 1993 (based on the budget-to-box office ratio), listed a little dinosaur movie called *Jurassic Park* as number two. Number one was Ang's film. But when we were making the film such an idea would have been dismissed as a lunatic prank. The idea that a gay-themed Chinese comedy made for less than one-thirtieth of the budget of an average Hollywood film would catch on with main-stream audiences all over the world was simply preposterous—at least to everyone but Ang, and he modestly kept his suspicions to himself.

And in a business where self-effacement and modesty are not exactly valued character traits, Ang has succeeded precisely because of his gentle yet determined demeanor. While the persona of the average producer or director is akin to something like a car salesman on an acid trip, it's difficult not to listen seriously to Ang because he speaks so softly and gestures so gently. On the film set during production Ang is, like the emotions his films elicit, everywhere and nowhere—his crews revere him even when they hardly notice that he's there giving the orders and providing the vision that's keeping them working night and day. For anyone even vaguely familiar with the norms of behavior in the film industry, Ang is a genuine anomaly, whose films express the quietly joyous working conditions under which he and his crews create them.

Of course, there are moments when the anonymous facade of the low-budget American independent filmmaker is removed. Imagine the American crew's response to the first night of shooting on *The Wedding Banquet* when a dozen Chinese press and camera crews showed up at location to film our filming. Or when, in a banquet room filled with 200 Chinese-American volunteer extras, actress May Chin entered to ear-piercing shrieks of delight from her assembled fans—to the crew, she was simply a girl who could drink any grip or electric under the table at our end of week bar hops, not the pop singing superstar she is in Taiwan.

For *Eat Drink Man Woman*, Ang returned to Taipei to make his first film there, coming back to New York for the post-production. Unlike his first two films, which took place in New York and were acted in a mixture of Chinese and English, *Eat Drink* is fully Taiwanese in flavor and content, based on a script developed by Taiwanese television writer Hui-Ling Wang. But even here Ang's transcontinental concerns are not far below the surface. The world outside Taiwan figures prominently in the lives of these characters— all culture these days is multi-culture—and Ang's life and art are a perfect reflection of the productive possibilities of that fact.

Writing screenplays in such a cultural stew is no easy feat. For each of the scripts printed here, first drafts were written in Chinese, then translated into English, re-written in English, translated back into Chinese, and eventually sub-titled in Chinese and English and a dozen other languages. The story of *The Wedding Banquet*, which rests on the assumption of linguistic misunderstanding, is an emblem of many of the problems and issues we all engaged as writers on the films. But the surprising coincidences and parallels we discovered during the writing process were equally enlightening. There was many a time when I, working with my American assumptions, would be re-working a scene and finding myself frustrated by Ang's insistence that the psychology of the characters I was sketching was not naturally Chinese. My initial inclination was to study even harder the Chinese poems, stories, and histories I had been accumulating as research, usually to no avail. Finally, in frustration, I'd simply give up and write the scenes as "Jewish" as I could make them. "Ah-ha," Ang would respond on reading the new draft. "Very Chinese!"

If the two scripts published here, along with the script for Ang Lee's first film, *Pushing Hands*, could be said to have a common theme, it is the question of the father, of the role of the patriarch in a world where the patriarchy is under justifiable fire. In one way, *The Wedding Banquet* is very much about making the institution of fatherhood safe for the contemporary world, while *Eat Drink Man Woman* is about contemporary fatherhood's comically disruptive attempts at reconfiguring itself.

The Wedding Banquet is based on a real person's existence—a Taiwanese son living in the States who really does box up his and his longtime companion's gay identity every time the folks come for a visit. From that premise, fleshed out in a first draft screenplay by Taiwanese journalist and satirist Neal Peng, we decided to imagine the emotional and societal transformations it would take to make that person's story a happy one. Our model for the script was very much the screwball comedies of the thirties and forties, what Stanley Cavell has called the comedies of "remarriage." In this case we had to split Wai-Tung and Simon apart, in order to bring them back, both as lovers and as "fathers"—as new versions of fatherhood. Taking the "perfect" heterosexual pairings of white Hollywood cinema and transmuting them into a "perfectly normal" gay and mixed-race couple was, we thought, going to be an enormous challenge. In fact, it proved to be the easy part of the script, as the civil marriage of hearts and minds Cavell has so richly explored appeared emblematic of gay coupledom (at least in one version) as we know it.

The trick of the script, however, was to sneak in the audience's sympathies with the characters—Mr. and Mrs. Gao—who through most of the film appeared to be the most secondary and reactionary. In writing the script, we tried to respect and to pay attention to the destiny and feelings of each of the characters, and the surprise of the film is not so much the "plot point" revealed at the end, but the fact that even the hippest viewers find themselves seeing the world through the Zen gaze of the father—a man whose desires are fulfilled through the subversion of the very traditions that instilled those desires in him in the first place.

Eat Drink takes the classical comedic formula—in which the sexuality of the younger generation poses a threat to the "senile" societal order, a threat disposed of through the channeling of youthful sexuality into the institution of marriage—and turns it on its head. Marriage functions in the script not so much as a longed-for state of equilibrium, but as a paradoxical escape route by which members of one family bail out in order to form new, equally fractious unions of desire and convenience. As in Shakespeare's later plays, the romances like *Winter's Tale* and *Pericles*, the script deals with the impossibility of comedy—although this impossibility is itself funny— in a world in which society's normal channelings of desire actually work against the grain of tradition and patriarchal order. If the classical, technical definition of comedy is a work which ends with a marriage (this is how Shakespeare's comedies were grouped together when first published), we posed ourselves the challenge of recreating a world in which the final marriage actually signifies Romance— you might call this Buddhist comedy.

In such a world, the laughter we seek to elicit is neither triumphantly normative nor derisively objectifying, but rather a thoughtful, human response to life's ever-changing circumstances.

James Schamus
New York City, May 1994

EAT DRINK
MAN WOMAN

The cast in alphabetical order:

Sylvia Chang	JIN-RONG
Winston Chao	LI KAI
Chao-Jung Chen	GUO LUN
Lester Chen	RAYMOND
Yu Chen	RACHEL
Ah-Leh Gua	MRS. LIANG
Chi-Der Hong	CLASS LEADER
Gin-Ming Hsu	COACH CHAI
Huei-Yi Lin	SISTER CHANG
Shih-Jay Lin	CHIEF'S SON
Chin-Cheng Lu	MING-DAO
Sihung Lung	MR. CHU
Cho-Gin Nei	AIRLINE SECRETARY
Yu-Chien Tang	SHAN-SHAN
Chung Ting	THE PRIEST
Cheng-Fen Tso	FAST FOOD MANAGER
Man-Sheng Tu	RESTAURANT MANAGER
Chuen Wang	CHIEF
Jui Wang	OLD WEN
Yu-Wen Wang	JIA-NING
Chien-Lien Wu	JIA-CHIEN
Hwa Wu	OLD MAN
Kuei-Mei Yang	JIA-JEN

EXTERIOR. TAIPEI STREETS. DAY.

Early afternoon traffic begins.

EXTERIOR. CHU STREET. DAY.

Looking down upon a quiet little home.

INTERIOR. CHU HOME KITCHEN. DAY.

Close on a pair of writhing fish, as the hands of old Mr. Chu, a master chef, pick up one of them and slice it open for cleaning.

The Chu kitchen is bright, with an island at its center. On the counter are an array of freshly bought ingredients—vegetables, intestines, herbs.

There is a multitude of kitchen utensils. The knives are laid out like an arsenal. Spices—some in big, some in little bottles—are shelved and neatly labeled like the canisters in a Chinese herbal pharmacy.

Already pots are bubbling, steam wafts from the bamboo steamers.

Mr. Chu goes out of the kitchen and down a gravel path to a chicken coop, where he fixes his gaze on a plump, red-feathered bird. When he re-enters the kitchen, he's holding onto a frantic, doomed chicken by the feet.

A montage follows of the various stages in the preparation and cooking of a meal—slicing vegetables, preparing a soup, adding spices.

Mr. Chu's intensity and mastery are evident in every move he makes.

The house is peaceful and calm as he works.

Mr. Chu washes out a chicken's stomach then mixes a stuffing with glutinous rice, red dates, ginseng, medlar, garlic and so on. Then like a surgeon, he takes a thread and sews up the belly. He puts it in a casserole and begins simmering it. Just as he finishes, the phone rings. He goes to answer it.

CHU

Hello. Yeah. Have you eaten? Not yet? Just throw together some noodles for lunch! That fish is excellent. Yeah! Yeah! Don't roast it, that would be a pity. It just needs to be lightly steamed. Don't add any salt. Whatever you do—no salt! Salt draws out the water in the fish, dries it out, then the flesh won't be tender. Listen, get a pot of boiling water for steaming, and pour salt around the edge of the plate . . .

There is a long pause in Mr. Chu's conversation.

> CHU
> . . . If not today, then when will we talk about it?

A pot boils over.

INTERIOR. BUS. DAY.

Jia-Jen, Mr. Chu's eldest daughter, rides on the bus on her way to church. She listens to swelling religious hymns over her Walkman. The Walkman momentarily conks out, but Jia-Jen fixes the problem with a few well-aimed taps of her hand.

INTERIOR. OFFICE. DAY.

A sleek, but nicely appointed, office with a view. The rest of the floor is deserted and half-dark—it's Sunday, and once again, Jia-Chien, Mr. Chu's middle daughter in her late twenties, is the only one at the office. She sits at a small computer, working intensely.

On the computer screen, we see a color display of a multi-media corporate presentation, showing airline routes and various charts of projected sales and profits.

Jia-Chien pauses to rub her eyes and lean back.

INTERIOR. AMERICAN STYLE FAST FOOD RESTAURANT. DAY.

Chicken patties are frying in hot oil. The pan is lifted up and they are separated into heating bins.

It's a Sunday and most of the customers are getting take-out. The employees go back and forth to the counter with fries and drinks, while in front of them, throngs of people come and go.

Jia-Ning, Mr. Chu's youngest daughter, is a twenty-year old university student. She is putting a piece of chicken on a tray.

> JIA-NING
> Small coke, three chickens? . . . That'll be 100 yuan.

> CUSTOMER
> *(pushing his way back to the front)*
> Hey, I ordered chicken!

Next to her is her friend Rachel, another student.

RACHEL
(looking inside the sandwich he thrusts at her)
That is chicken!

He's immediately swallowed up in a sea of customers.

Rachel and Jia-Ning trade a few words with each other over the roar of cash registers and people.

RACHEL
(bagging an order)
Oh, Jia-Ning, I forgot to tell you, I can't cover for you this afternoon. Guo-Lun decided he can take me to the beach after all.

JIA-NING
(scooping fries)
But you have to! Father will kill me if I'm late for Sunday dinner again. And I thought you and Guo-Lun broke up!

RACHEL
(reaching down for some ketchup)
We did! I just thought I'd torture him for a few more dates!

JIA-NING
(reaching down to speak to her)
Then why not torture him by keeping him waiting for an hour?

RACHEL
Great idea!

The Manager eyes them as he walks by.

                                        MANAGER
    Hurry up!

They smile.

INTERIOR. CHU KITCHEN. DAY.

Mr. Chu continues preparing for the Sunday feast.

INTERIOR. OFFICE. DAY.

*Jia-Chien looks at her watch, then reaches for the phone and dials. She speaks
into the phone.*

                                        JIA-CHIEN
    How's the new boyfriend?

                                        GRACE
                                      (voice off)
    Hi, Jia-Chien. Working again on a Sunday? New boyfriend's OK, pretty
    quiet. Especially after Bo-Kang.

                                        JIA-CHIEN
    Sounds good.

                                        GRACE
                                      (voice off)
    You wanna get together tonight? Don't be such a company slave.

                                        JIA-CHIEN
    Thanks, but I'm hooking up with Raymond later.

                                        GRACE
                                      (voice off)
    Raymond, eh? Heh-heh-heh.

                                        JIA-CHIEN
    What does that mean—''heh, heh, heh''?

INTERIOR. EVANGELICAL CHURCH. DAY.

Jia-Jen watches the Minister speaking.

                                        MINISTER
    The difference between Christians and ordinary people is not only do
    we have eternal hope, but we also rely on God to give us wisdom to

overcome our difficulties and to give us joyfulness and peace to settle our frustrations.

INTERIOR. RAYMOND'S APARTMENT. DAY.

The shades are drawn. Jia-Chien and Raymond are in the last throes of their lovemaking.

INTERIOR. CHU KITCHEN. DAY.

Mr. Chu blows air inside a boiled chicken and then bastes it.

INTERIOR. RAYMOND'S APARTMENT. DAY.

Raymond comes back into the bedroom with a drink of water, as Jia-Chien puts her shirt on.

He strokes her back.

> RAYMOND

You ok?

> JIA-CHIEN

Yeah. Just a little wound up. Work, you know, and the sale just closed on the apartment—all my savings, but it'll be worth it to get out of that house.

> RAYMOND
> *(kissing the back of her neck, watching her dress)*

That was wonderful.

> JIA-CHIEN

Yes.

> RAYMOND

Better than when we were together.

> JIA-CHIEN
> *(she smiles)*

It's so much easier with you now.

> RAYMOND
> *(laughing)*

We were something of a disaster as a couple, weren't we? My God, the shouting and fighting.

She is finished dressing, and comes over to him to plant a good-bye kiss on his forehead.

RAYMOND
Hey, you want to come down to my gallery now? A new show by a woman artist. I think you'd like her work.

JIA-CHIEN
I have to get home for the Sunday dinner torture ritual.

EXTERIOR. CHU BACKYARD. DAY.

Mr. Chu spoons out a spice from one of his many jars.

INTERIOR. FAST FOOD RESTAURANT. DAY.

As Jia-Ning walks out of the dressing room the Manager quickly runs by.

MANAGER
Hey, remember to punch your time card.

JIA-NING
(handing it to her)
You won't forget to change my Sunday schedule?

MANAGER
I'll see what I can do.

EXTERIOR. FAST FOOD RESTAURANT. DAY.

Jia-Ning looks across the street to find Guo-Lun standing against a wall, reading from a book. He's cute, overserious, bohemian-looking. She crosses to him.

JIA-NING
Hi, Guo-Lun!

He doesn't appear to recognize her.

GUO-LUN
Oh. Hi.

JIA-NING
I'm Chu Jia-Ning.

GUO-LUN
Oh . . .

JIA-NING
Rachel asked me to tell you she'll be an hour late.

GUO-LUN

Shit! How can she do this to me?

JIA-NING

Don't be angry! It's just an hour—even less now, really.

GUO-LUN

It's not the first time she's made a fool out of me.

JIA-NING

Don't take it too seriously.

GUO-LUN

What do you know? Have you ever been in love with someone who hated you? Someone who tried to hurt you every day?

JIA-NING
(trying to hide a smile)

It's my fault really. She forgot that she'd promised to cover for me, and I forced her to keep her promise. I didn't know I'd be the cause of so much suffering.

GUO-LUN
(hardly paying attention to her)

You're not the cause of anything, it's me. If only I could end my disgusting addiction to love, but the flames of my passion are too strong.

JIA-NING

Well, I'd better be going.

GUO-LUN

Okay, bye.

He opens his book and begins to read again with a huff.

JIA-NING
(pausing)

Will you wait for her? When you see Rachel could you remind her to bring back the red shirt she borrowed from me—she can just bring it to work on Wednesday?

GUO-LUN
(hardly acknowledging her)

Whatever.

JIA-NING
(again pausing)

What are you reading?

GUO-LUN
(annoyed, without looking up)

Dostoyevski.

JIA-NING

Oh. Bye.

She steals a glance at him as she walks away.

INTERIOR. CHU KITCHEN. EVENING.

Mr. Chu is cooking in a wok. On a nearby wall hangs a faded black and white photograph of an elegant woman who bears a close resemblance to Jia-Chien.

EXTERIOR. IN FRONT OF CHU HOUSE. EVENING.

Sister Chang's cycle moped drives up with Jia-Jen riding on the back seat. Jia-Jen gets off.

JIA-JEN

Thank you!

SISTER CHANG

Now you promise me—next time you'll let me take you to choir practice?

JIA-JEN

I'll think about it.

SISTER CHANG

Listen, Brother Chai is the handsomest man in the congregation—and he's told me how much he admires your voice!

JIA-JEN

Sister Chang, I don't wish to be liked only for my voice!

SISTER CHANG
(driving off)

I'll never find a husband for you!

JIA-JEN
(not really talking to be heard)

Then stop trying!

EXTERIOR. CORNER. EVENING.

Jia-Ning steps down off a bus.

EXTERIOR. CHU STREET. EVENING.

Raymond drops Jia-Chien off. She watches him drive off in his fancy sports car.

EXTERIOR. CHU BACKYARD. EVENING.

Mr. Chu takes a duck out of the roaster and admires it.

EXTERIOR. CHU BACKYARD. LATER.

Karaoke music from a neighboring house blasts into the Chu's. The neighbors are belting it out in typical out-of-key splendor.

INTERIOR. CHU FAMILY DINING ROOM. EVENING.

Close up, with music up:

An array of perfectly cooked dishes spread out on the dinner table. The camera moves back to reveal:

The three Chu sisters, all looking at the food with various degrees of disinterest.

JIA-JEN
(prays more or less to herself)

Dear God, please bring luck to our family, and I want to thank you so much for this terrific dinner, and I want to thank you again for bringing our family together with happiness. In the name of Jesus Christ, thank you. Amen.

On Mr. Chu, as he stands briefly before his latest masterwork, and then takes his seat.

They eat silently for a bit.

MR. CHU

These past two days I . . .

Jia-Chien grimaces a bit as she tastes the soup. Mr. Chu notices and pauses.

MR. CHU

Something the matter?

JIA-CHIEN

No, it's fine.

She tastes it again, lets it swish around on her tongue.

MR. CHU
(getting defensive)

Hm?

JIA-CHIEN

Nothing.

MR. CHU

Say it!

The other two daughters are looking a bit nervous—this is an oft-repeated scene.

JIA-CHIEN

This braised chicken soup with shark's fin . . . it feels like . . . the ham
which you used to stew the shark's fin into the chicken soup is a bit old.

MR. CHU

Hmpf!

JIA-NING

It's fine!

JIA-JEN

Father probably forgot to taste it.

JIA-CHIEN

Or his sense of taste getting worse again.

MR. CHU

My tongue is fine!

Mr. Chu gets up and walks into the kitchen.

JIA-JEN

Yesterday—

JIA-NING
(overlapping)

—Our school . . . You first.

JIA-JEN

Yesterday Jin-Feng called from America! Her mother wants to come
back.

Mr. Chu is in the kitchen, listening.

JIA-CHIEN

Wasn't she waiting for her green card?

JIA-JEN

Yes, but she can't stay there anymore. Jin-Feng and Mrs. Liang have
been arguing for a long time. Last time, the police even came to the
door!

JIA-NING

Wow! Mrs. Liang is really hell on wheels!

JIA-JEN

It's not surprising that she can't get used to living there. The language problem. . . . and she can't find a mah-jong companion. . . . Plus, her son-in-law isn't Chinese—it's surprising she didn't come back sooner.

JIA-CHIEN

Still, it might be all right for Jin-Rong to have her here—she'll be able to take care of Shan-Shan.

JIA-NING

Then again, it might make her life even more stressful!

JIA-CHIEN

I'm sure it will work out fine. And Dad will have someone in the neighborhood to gossip with.

MR. CHU

Like I have so much time after taking care of you three to keep someone company while they gossip? *(pause)* These past two days . . .

Again he notices Jia-Chien, this time chewing slowly on her beef.

MR. CHU

What now?

JIA-CHIEN

Well, I have a little announcement . . . Have you seen those TV commercials for "Little Paris in the East?" That new luxury apartment building in Hsin-Den?

No response.

JIA-CHIEN

A friend of mine, who knows the contractors, told me how the building is solid and well built. He was able to get my bid in for a good price. You know, for an apartment—

JIA-NING

You're moving out!

JIA-CHIEN

Not immediately, of course—the building is still under construction. I've put most of my savings down for the deposit, and—

MR. CHU
(looking pissed off)
That's good. Real estate is a smart investment these days.

JIA-CHIEN
(formally asking him)
Then I'll move out when the apartment is ready?

The phone rings. Jia-Ning goes to get it.

JIA-NING
Hello? Dad, it's for you.

MR. CHU
Hello? Huh? Right away!

Mr. Chu throws down the phone and rushes out of the room. The girls watch him.

EXTERIOR. ALLEY NEXT TO CHU FAMILY HOUSE. MORNING.

Mr. Chu hastily comes out the door, pulling on his jacket. He yells back.

MR̃. CHU
There are crab dumplings in the steamer! Get them out when you're
ready to eat them!

He walks quickly down the alley to the street.

INTERIOR. DINING ROOM. NIGHT.

The three daughters sit around the table. No one eats.

EXTERIOR. TAIPEI SKYLINE. NIGHT.

The city is lit up with glorious neon colors.

INTERIOR. GRAND HOTEL RESTAURANT. NIGHT.

Mr. Chu hops out of a taxi and hurries through an enormous and elegant lobby.

INTERIOR. BANQUET HALL KITCHEN. NIGHT.

*Mr. Chu pushes open two doors. There's a burst of light and suddenly we're in a
commotion filled kitchen.*

The Manager keeps the pressure on.

MANAGER

Hurry! Get the assorted jumbo sea cucumbers now!

The kitchen is frenetic with activity and noise. Cooks, waiters, assistants, bus boys—scores of people scampering about the crowded area chopping, stirring, pouring, carrying dishes.

ASSISTANT
(off screen)

Master Chu is here!

The Manager looks as though his prayers to heaven have been answered. He corners Mr. Chu.

MANAGER

Thank the lucky stars, you've come!

Mr. Chu vigorously washes his hands and puts on a cook's hat. The Manager helps him tie on his apron.

MR. CHU

Where's Old Wen?

OLD WEN
(other side of kitchen)

Over here! What a mess, eh?

MANAGER

The boss wanted the banquet tonight to be perfect. Now look at the mess . . .

MR. CHU

The menu?

MANAGER

The menu!

The Manager hands Mr. Chu a menu. Old Wen pulls out his own glasses and hands them to Mr. Chu. Mr. Chu with one glance knows exactly what to do.

MR. CHU

It's all right. The last four courses are stews; all we have to do is get the Whole Shark Fin done and there's no problem.

MANAGER

With you here, I can relax. I'm handing the whole mess over to you. I'm going out front to see how things are going.

The Manager leaves.

OLD WEN

It's the Whole Shark Fin with Green Vegetable dish! The guy who went to buy the ingredients didn't know what he was doing. When he was soaking the fins, the color was fine! Who could have guessed that when they were put in the pot, they'd fall apart.

Mr. Chu walks over to the pot and looks inside. He frowns.

MR. CHU

These are fake!

All the cooks in the kitchen crowd around.

MR. CHU

As soon as fake fins go into hot water, they don't have any elasticity. After steaming for awhile, they come apart. The flavor won't go in, no matter how long you cook them.

OLD WEN

What are we going to do now? The General's son is getting married. The place is filled with big shots.

MR. CHU

This is only good for gravy. In Whole Shark Fin with Green Vegetable it will make the whole dish look like porcupine. *(He thinks)* We'll turn it into Joy Luck Dragon Phoenix.

OLD WEN

Joy Luck Dragon Phoenix? But how?

MR. CHU

I don't know, but I will by the time the dish is ready.

OLD WEN

All right! Get me lobster! Jade Prawns! Abalone!

The Chief Assistant goes to serve the guests. The cooks run to their places and begin preparations.

INTERIOR. KITCHEN. NIGHT.

Jia-Ning, Jia-Jen, and Jia-Chien are cleaning up the kitchen and doing the dishes.

JIA-CHIEN

. . . On the tenth floor, the windows face south.

JIA-NING

Central air conditioning?

JIA-CHIEN

Of course! And there's going to be a guest room, so you can come and stay whenever you like.

Jia-Jen pauses over the dishes, upset, on the verge of tears.

JIA-NING

What is it?

JIA-JEN

I'm sorry—I don't know why I'm upset. I should be happy for her.

JIA-CHIEN
(in a friendly tone)

No you're not—and I understand. I shouldn't leave Father in your hands, but I just can't live here with him any more. Even though I'll be just a few miles away, I'll really be in another world. You have every reason to be upset with me.

JIA-NING

Why should we be upset? If you were getting married—or Jia-Jen were getting married for that matter—there'd be nothing but celebration.

JIA-JEN

I'm sorry if I'm acting upset—I just wonder how Father will take it.

JIA-CHIEN

Please! He can barely stand the sight of me these days—neither of us can sneeze without starting a fight. It will be a great relief for everyone. . . . No, Father doesn't need us around—what he really needs is a relationship with someone his own age—*(cracking a joke)* Like Mrs. Liang, for example!

JIA-JEN

That's not even funny.

JIA-NING

We've tried to set him up with other ladies before, and it's always been a disaster—it's obvious he only had one true love in his life, and that was our mother.

JIA-CHIEN

Hah, you call that love? All the bickering and fighting.

JIA-JEN

What can you remember of their relationship? Maybe it didn't adhere to your modern notions of romance, but it was founded on real old-fashioned respect and values.

JIA-CHIEN

It was an old-fashioned war, that ended only when mom died!

JIA-JEN

How could you know—you were just a kid when she died.

JIA-CHIEN

I was old enough to know her better than you ever did!

JIA-NING

Stop it, you two.

INTERIOR. BANQUET HALL KITCHEN. NIGHT—CONTINUED.

Mr. Chu has personally taken charge, adding ingredients to the shark fin soup.

MR. CHU

Try it.

Old Wen stands beside him, carefully testing the flavor.

MR. CHU

Hm?

Old Wen jokingly makes a face of disgust, but then nods and smiles. It tastes amazing.

MR. CHU

There you go.

INTERIOR. BANQUET HALL. NIGHT.

The banquet guests taste the revived soup, as the Manager worriedly looks on for an indication of the soup's success. Sure enough, the banquet guests like it. The Manager sighs in relief.

INTERIOR. CHU KITCHEN. NIGHT.

Jia-Jen is finishing up the cleaning alone. She opens the steamer and looks at the little steamed crab dumplings and wrinkles her nose.

From the living room comes the sound of Jia-Ning's voice.

JIA-NING

Jin-Rong is here!

JIA-JEN

Oh! *(she wipes her hands)* Hi.

Jin-Rong, mid-thirties, pleasant but harried looking, sticks her head in the kitchen.

JIN-RONG
Hi. I thought you'd all be here. Where's Mr. Chu . . . ?

JIA-JEN
Something came up at the restaurant and he went over to help. Jia-Chien is holed up in her room. Have you eaten?

> JIN-RONG

It's eight o'clock. How could I still be hungry?

Shan-Shan, a little girl of eight, Jin-Rong's daughter, enters the kitchen.

> SHAN-SHAN

Today Ma grilled the fish to nothing.

> JIN-RONG

Hey! I didn't bring you along to complain.

> JIA-JEN

Wait a minute and I'll give you some of Mr. Chu's crab dumplings to take home.

> JIA-NING

You got a haircut!

> JIN-RONG

Every day I'm running around like crazy. I don't have time to fix myself up. I figured it was best to cut it off.

> JIA-NING

It makes you look younger!

> JIN-RONG

Does it? I thought it would make me look more professional.

Shan-Shan tugs at Jia-Ning's sleeve.

> SHAN-SHAN

Can we go drawing now?

Jia-Ning and Shan-Shan go off together.

INTERIOR. JIA-NING'S ROOM. NIGHT.

Jia-Ning is drawing a cartoon on a computer while holding Shan-Shan in her lap.

EXTERIOR. GARDEN. NIGHT.

Jia-Jen and Jin-Rong are sitting on the porch.

> JIA-JEN

Was it really that bad?

> JIN-RONG

Who knows? They were both crying and fussing. My mother said Jin-Feng wasn't being filial. Jin-Feng was saying that if my mother continued to live with them, she'd end up divorced. I thought to myself, if it comes down to Jin-Feng having to get a divorce, my mother really couldn't take it.

JIA-JEN

But really Jin-Feng ought to be taking care of her. What a situation. You're selling insurance and taking care of a child, and meanwhile you have your own divorce to deal with!

JIN-RONG

And now that's going from bad to worse! You know he's hired private detectives to follow me!

JIA-JEN

Really?

JIN-RONG

He will do anything to take Shan-Shan away from me. I simply can't wait for the final decree.

JIA-JEN

And on top of this, your mother's moving in!

JIN-RONG

What can I do! You and Jin-Feng are old schoolmates. You know her. My mother's always wanted to be with me instead of her.

JIA-JEN

Actually, our situation's more or less the same. My father will want to live with me forever.

JIN-RONG

It's not the same. Mr. Chu is much better than my Ma. He can take care of himself and others. Not like my Ma.

JIA-JEN

It's not true! How many Sunday dinners like this can we have? Jia-Ning is still young. Jia-Chien will do whatever she wants, and it will be up to me to take care of Dad for the rest of my life.

JIN-RONG

He probably doesn't want it to end up like that.

Shan-Shan has crept up to the two of them. Suddenly the cartoon is in front of them.

SHAN-SHAN

Mama, look at this! Jia-Ning drew Mr. Chu!

Jin-Rong and Jia-Jen smile at the drawing.

> JIN-RONG
>
> It's about time to go home.

> JIA-JEN
>
> Wait, I'll get the dumplings for you.

> JIN-RONG
>
> Please don't. We're always taking food home.

> JIA-JEN
>
> Don't worry about it, you're like another daughter in this family . . .
> *(to Shan-Shan)* So you really are like Mr. Chu's granddaughter.

> SHAN-SHAN
>
> I want to show this to Mr. Chu!

> JIA-NING
>
> Hey, Shan-Shan!

She chases Shan-Shan through the yard.

INTERIOR. JIA-CHIEN'S ROOM. SAME TIME.

Jia-Chien works on a portable computer.

> SHAN-SHAN
>
> I want to show this to Mr. Chu! I want to show this to Mr. Chu! I want to
> show this to Mr. Chu!

She overhears Shan-Shan's laughter, then goes back to her work.

> SHAN-SHAN
>
> Bet you can't catch me!

INTERIOR. BANQUET HALL KITCHEN. NIGHT.

*Old Wen and Mr. Chu sit on some cartons, next to the dumpster, and share a
bottle of rice wine.*

Old Wen is constantly offering Mr. Chu more wine.

*Two Kitchen Helpers come out and start dumping huge amounts of delicious
looking food into the dumpster—lobsters, steamed dumplings. Mr. Chu looks on
in disgust.*

MR. CHU

Hey, those dumplings haven't been touched. Why don't you take some
of that home to your kids?

HELPER
(walking back in)
Why don't YOU take it home to YOUR kids?

Mr. Chu, pissed, is about to respond, but just goes back to his drink.

OLD WEN

Old Chu, don't get upset. Girls have to leave home eventually. It was
bound to happen.

MR. CHU

Why should I be upset? I hope they all to move out so I can have a quiet
life.

OLD WEN

Quiet life? I know you. What you want, you can't get. And what you
don't want, you can't get rid of. You're as repressed as a turtle. That old
maid of yours Jia-Jen will stick to you for life whether you want her to
or not—unless you can marry her off!

MR.CHU

Marry who? Since she lost her college asshole boyfriend she's never
looked at another man. You know that.

OLD WEN

And now she has the perfect boyfriend—Jesus Christ—Ha!

MR. CHU

Don't make fun of her religion! *(casting a sideways glance at Old Wen)* How is it that for thirty years I have put up with this kind of talk from you?

OLD WEN

Be thankful someone's around to tell you the truth.

MR. CHU

That Jia-Chien's temper—I can't take it anymore.

OLD WEN

It's because that girl's a perfect blend of you and her mother—exactly half of each of you. Her mother's stubbornness and willfulness, and your pickiness and pomposity!

Mr. Chu laughs.

OLD WEN

And that's exactly like YOU! I think I know her better than you do.

MR. CHU

I don't understand any of them, and I don't want to know. Let them grow up and leave. It's like cooking. You lose your appetite when the dish is done.

They drink again.

OLD WEN

At least people like your cooking.

MR. CHU

In fact, without you, Old Wen, I'd have to give up even that. With hardly any taste buds of my own any more, I have only your face to judge my recipes by.

OLD WEN

Don't be silly! You're still the greatest chef in Taipei. Like a great composer who's gone deaf— that Bay- Bay-

MR. CHU

—Beethoven.

OLD WEN

Beethoven. That is right, so the good sound doesn't come in the ear, the good taste doesn't in the mouth and the good sex . . . God knows where. . . .

MR.CHU

You're drunk.

Cut To:

INTERIOR. GRAND HOTEL HALLWAY. LATER.

Mr. Chu and Old Wen stagger out of the kitchen.

MR. CHU

Eat drink, man woman—nourishment and sex. The basic human desires. There's no avoiding them! All my life, every day, that's all I've ever done. It pisses me off—is that all there is to life?

OLD WEN

We're still alive, still cooking, thank God. What about your recipes?

MR. CHU

What recipes?

OLD WEN

You told me you want to write down the recipes in your head. In case one day . . .

Old Wen draws his finger across his throat like a knife.

MR. CHU

God damn you! Are you counting the days 'til I die?

Mr. Chu pretends to fart into his hand and then puts it in front of Old Wen's face.

MR. CHU

Here, taste this!

The both of them laugh as they continue walking down the hallway drunkenly.

INTERIOR. JIA-NING'S ROOM. MORNING.

Mr. Chu, wearing a jogging suit, stands outside her door.

MR. CHU

Little daughter?

He pushes open the door and looks in at Jia-Ning who is sound asleep.

> MR. CHU
>
> It's six o'clock!

Jia-Ning lets out a sleepy yawn.

Mr. Chu, now impatient, calls to her again.

> MR. CHU
>
> Get up, lazy-bones!

INTERIOR. JIA-CHIEN'S ROOM. MORNING.

Mr. Chu knocks on her door. It swings open, to discover Jia-Chien slumped over her desk, the computer next to her head.

He coughs loudly to wake her up.

> MR. CHU
>
> Jia-Chien, get up!

She stirs awake.

> MR. CHU
>
> How many times have I told you that you shouldn't fall asleep at your desk like that. It's bad for your posture.

> JIA-CHIEN
>
> And didn't the doctor tell you that jogging was bad for your back?

> MR. CHU
>
> Hmpf.

EXTERIOR. STREET. MORNING.

Mr. Chu listlessly jogs along a path in a park. His rhythm uneven. He passes several people who are also exercising, and stops to catch his breath. He then forces himself to go on.

EXTERIOR. BUS STOP. MORNING.

Shan-Shan stands at the bus stop with a line of other students. She's eating a dumpling from a plastic bag.

Mr. Chu runs past and then stops.

> MR. CHU
>
> Shan-Shan!

SHAN-SHAN

Good morning, Mr. Chu!

MR. CHU

Good morning! Off to school? How come you're eating your breakfast
out here in the street?

SHAN-SHAN

I've got to get to school early. There's no time for breakfast. Look!
These are the dumplings you made yesterday.

Mr. Chu looks surprised.

SHAN-SHAN

Ma squeezed the juice out so I wouldn't get my hands all greasy.

MR. CHU

At lunch time I want you to come to my house. I'm going to make you
lunch.

SHAN-SHAN

I have to stay at school all day.

MR. CHU

All day! Where's your lunch box?

Shan-Shan pulls some money from her pocket.

SHAN-SHAN

The bus is here!

*Mr. Chu watches as Shan-Shan stuffs the dumpling back in the plastic bag and
pushes against an adult's behind as she squeezes into the bus.*

INTERIOR. TECHNICAL HIGH SCHOOL CLASSROOM. DAY.

Jia-Jen is lecturing about chemical equations to a class of bored students.

JIA-JEN

The valence electron of a typical element is equal to its groups . . . its
valence electron is equal to its groups. Any questions?

She walks over to the other side of the blackboard.

JIA-JEN

Okay, let's look at the periodic table of the elements again. These are all
Group A elements. 1A, 2A, 3A, —

Suddenly, one of her students bangs his head on a table after dozing off. The entire class laughs.

JIA-JEN

Pay attention! 4A, 5A, 6A, 7A, 8A. Now let's look at 1A.

The moment she turns to the blackboard, the students at the back start passing notes around. Suddenly a volleyball flies up from the court below and bounces into the classroom.

JIA-JEN
(frowning)

Who will return the ball?

Everyone in the class raises their hand in unison.

STUDENTS

I'll go.

JIA-JEN

Very well, then I'll do it.

Jia-Jen picks up the ball and carries it over to the edge of the open corridor.

The Class Leader immediately stands up, looking for the missing love letter.

CLASS LEADER

Where'd it go? Give it back to me!

INTERIOR. OPEN CORRIDOR. DAY.

Holding the ball, Jia-Jen looks over the railing and sees a volleyball game going on in the court below. The young volleyball instructor looks up at her very apologetically. He is definitely a hunk.

MING-DAO

Sorry! Sorry! We don't know our own strength down here!

JIA-JEN
(bashful)

It's all right.

She continues to hold the ball.

MING-DAO

I'll come up and get it.

JIA-JEN

Not necessary. I can throw it down.

Jia-Jen drops the ball and Ming-Dao catches it like a suitor receiving a bouquet of flowers after a serenade. The student volleyball players cheer.

PLAYERS
She's throwing the bouquet! He caught the bouquet!

Jia-Jen turns red. Ming-Dao laughs and gives Jia-Jen a bow of great thanks. He returns to the court and continues his class.

INTERIOR. TECHNICAL HIGH SCHOOL ROOM. DAY.

Jia-Jen returns to the classroom. The rowdy classroom gets instantaneously quiet as she enters.

She addresses the Class Leader.

JIA-JEN
What's going on? Class Leader, what have you got in your hand?

CLASS LEADER
I don't have anything.

Some of the students giggle.

JIA-JEN
Bring it here, let me see it.

CLASS LEADER

There's nothing worth seeing, Teacher.

JIA-JEN

Bring it here!

Jia-Jen walks over to the Class Leader's desk. He stands up. He's a good head taller than she is.

JIA-JEN

Just sit down! Give it to me!

The Class Leader has no choice but to hand it over.

Jia-Jen looks at it.

JIA-JEN

Writing love letters in chemistry class?

ANOTHER STUDENT

Love letters are a kind of chemical catalyst!

Everyone laughs.

CLASS LEADER

Someone wrote it to me!

JIA-JEN

What's the difference! They're sickening! There's no place for this in class! You're showing off. Who hasn't received love letters before?

Jia-Jen crumples the letter and throws it away, continuing with the lesson. The Class Leader is crushed.

INTERIOR. FRENCH LANGUAGE REVIEW CLASS. DAY.

University students with earphones on are repeating their French lessons.

Jia-Ning's heart isn't in the lesson, but she repeats the phrases anyhow. They're from Apollinaire's "Zone."

STUDENTS

"A la fin tu es las de ce monde ancien Bergère ô tour Eiffel le troupeau des ponts bêle ce matin . . ."

EXTERIOR. UNIVERSITY CAMPUS. DAY.

Jia-Ning walks past one of the buildings after class.

EXTERIOR. CHU'S BACK YARD. DAY.

The washing machine spins to a stop. Mr. Chu gets out the clothes to hang them up to dry. The girls have lots of silk garments that have gotten all tangled up together. It takes Mr. Chu forever to separate them out.

INTERIOR. AIRLINE OFFICE CONFERENCE ROOM. DAY.

A group of executives sits around a conference table. Jia-Chien is the only woman among them. She stands before them, finishing her presentation.

JIA-CHIEN

There is no question that with the American airlines going out of business, now is the time. In particular, we should fight hard for the Sydney and the Bangkok routes, which the British are also eyeing—we can expect them to be our toughest competition here . . .

The door opens, and someone slips into the darkened meeting room.

JIA-CHIEN

I'll be able to put a price on most of these routes within two weeks, but overall my impression is that there is significant potential in almost all of them.

Jia-Chien turns on the lights, picks up her papers and goes back to her seat.

CHIEF

Good. Thank you Deputy Director Chu for that report. It's obvious to me that this plan poses real opportunities for growth of our company—

CHIEF'S SON

—But do we have enough planes for all these cities?

CHIEF

Shut up, you idiot.

The Chief's son, frustrated, runs from the room.

CHIEF
(embarrassed)

My son just graduated. He'll figure out what's—*(noticing Li-Kai)* Ah! Our chief negotiator! Welcome! Everyone, please welcome Li-Kai—the man who single-handedly got us our Amsterdam routes.

There is light applause from around the room.

CHIEF

Thank goodness you're here to take charge of these new negotiations!

LI-KAI

My apologies for being late—my flight was delayed.

CHIEF

(a pause—he doesn't know how to take this remark)

Hah, hah. Always kidding, eh? Well, we have a big battle to wage, and he is our general. I want everyone here to extend to Li Kai the utmost courtesy and cooperation. Whatever he wants he gets.

During the speech, Li-Kai has caught the eye of Jia-Chien, who blushingly trades his glance for a moment.

INTERIOR. TECHNICAL HIGH SCHOOL CLASSROOM. DAY.

Jia-Jen continues to teach the same class of students.

JIA-JEN

By following this rule, you see the energy of the chemical element getting higher and higher.

A distant school bell rings.

JIA-JEN

Go home and study hard. Class dismissed.

CLASS LEADER

Attention.

All the students stand up.

CLASS LEADER

Stand straight. Bow.

STUDENTS

Thank you, teacher.

After class, Jia-Jen leaves the classroom and the Class Leader hurriedly gets the crumpled letter from the wastebasket as the other students gather around him.

INTERIOR. BALL COURT SIDELINES. DAY.

Jia-Jen stops to watch the game. She sees that Ming-Dao has divided the class into teams. He has joined one team, and nods hello to her as the game starts. He gets the ball and spikes it. When he does this, his whole attitude is one of great self-pride. Getting a point, he shouts and slaps a high-five just like one of the students.

Jia-Jen walks on. Suddenly, there is a yell behind her, and everyone congregates in the middle of the court.

JIA-JEN
(running back)

What happened?

PLAYERS

Our coach dislocated his shoulder.

JIA-JEN

Dislocated?

MING-DAO
(wincing, in great pain)

My right shoulder always goes.

JIA-JEN

We've got to get you to a hospital!

MING-DAO

They've gone to get Coach Chai.

JIA-JEN

What for?

The students have already returned with Coach Chai.

CHAI

What's happened? Out again? Come on!

He takes Ming-Dao's shoulder and wrenches it back.

Ming-Dao lets out a cry of pain, then suddenly breaks into a stupid grin.

MING-DAO

Wow!

He shakes and wiggles a bit.

MING-DAO

Thanks, Coach Chai! It's as good as new. C'mon, let's keep going!

CHAI

Don't be an idiot. Lay off it for today. Everyone, that's it! Break it up.

The students move the net, take the ball, and disperse. Jia-Jen, seeing that things are okay, leaves.

INTERIOR. CHU FAMILY'S KITCHEN. DAY.

Mr. Chu is busy chopping and frying.

Mr. Chu opens a cabinet and gets out a red lacquer food case. It has four layers with bamboo cases inside that help keep food warm.

EXTERIOR. ELEMENTARY SCHOOL ENTRANCE. DAY.

Fast food trucks have already filled up the parking spaces outside the gates of the school.

The school bell sounds. Every vendor of every truck is waiting for that brief moment of peace before the tidal wave.

Suddenly a mass of elementary students rush to the metal gates and thrust out their hands, shouting their orders. The vendors are all busy taking money and passing the lunches.

Mr. Chu enters and walks past the commotion.

INTERIOR. CLASSROOM. DAY.

Mr. Chu greets Shan's teacher who is sitting at the front of the class.

> MR. CHU
> Teacher, I'm bringing Shan-Shan her lunch box.

He goes to where Shan-Shan is sitting. He pushes aside the lunch she's bought and opens up what he's brought.

> MR. CHU
> I didn't have much time to make you more than a few small dishes. Spare Ribs, Crab with Vegetables, Shrimp with Green Peas, Bean Sprouts and Sliced Chicken. This is your favorite, Bitter Melon Soup. I didn't want to make too much because I was afraid you wouldn't be able to finish it all.

Mr. Chu arranges the four dishes and the soup and looks at wide-eyed Shan-Shan.

> MR. CHU
> Come on, eat while it's hot.

Mr. Chu turns his head and discovers that many of Shan-Shan's classmates have crowded around and are staring at the four course meal on her desk.

EXTERIOR. OUTSIDE THE GATES OF THE TECHNICAL HIGH SCHOOL. DAY.

High school students are pouring out of the school at the end of the day. Jia-Jen, wearing a Walkman, is humming along to one of her religious hymns.

Jia-Jen is shocked to see Ming-Dao, on a motorcycle, stop in front of her. She sees his smile and his lips move but can't hear what he's saying. It takes her a while before she realizes the problem and pulls off the headphones.

JIA-JEN

I'm so sorry!

MING-DAO

Are you catching a bus?

JIA-JEN

Your shoulder? You can still ride—

MING-DAO

No problem. Tomorrow, I'll be able to spike the ball. Next week's the big tournament.

JIA-JEN

Somehow, we've never met before.

MING-DAO

I've just recently joined the staff to coach the volleyball team. I'm Chou Ming Dao.

JIA-JEN

Chu Jia-Jen.

MING-DAO

Where do you live?

JIA-JEN

Ho-Pei East Road.

MING-DAO

That's a nice area!

JIA-JEN

It's an old house.

MING-DAO

I would have given you a ride if it were on the way.

JIA-JEN

It's easy on the bus.

MING-DAO

Well, I'm off. Come root for the team next week!

Jia-Jen nods her head.

Ming-Dao very smoothly turns the motorcycle in a half-circle, zigzags off, waving his hand.

Jia-Jen waves back and then continues on as before, holding tightly to her books.

EXTERIOR. RESTAURANT. DAY.

Jia-Ning spots Guo-Lun across the street. She crosses to him.

JIA-NING

Hi! What are you doing here?

GUO-LUN

What do you think? I'm waiting for Rachel, who will no doubt keep me waiting another hour.

JIA-NING

I doubt it!

GUO-LUN

How do you know?

JIA-NING

Because she got off work over an hour ago. She told me she was going home.

Guo-Lun looks like a cow in line to be slaughtered.

INTERIOR. NOODLE STAND. DAY.

Guo-Lun and Jia-Ning are seated, as she eats and he morosely looks on.

>   JIA-NING
> Try this. It tastes great.

>   GUO-LUN
> The smell is making me sick.

>   JIA-NING
> You're just feeling sorry for yourself.

>   GUO-LUN
> Actually, I feel wonderful—love is suffering, and I know she truly loves
> me at heart.

>   JIA-NING
> But she told me she doesn't love you at all.

>   GUO-LUN
> She doesn't love me? Then how come she expends so much energy
> torturing me?

>   JIA-NING
> But that isn't true love at all! You two hardly know each other—you
> hardly even talk to each other. When was the last time you had a real
> conversation—about your feelings, about life?

>   GUO-LUN
> I can't remember, it's such a blur.

>   JIA-NING
> I'll tell you what's a blur—your idea of love! True love is being with
> someone who lets you really express your feelings, around whom you
> feel free to talk about anything.

>   GUO-LUN
> Well, I feel free to talk about my feelings around you, so is that true
> love?

Jia-Ning blushes.

>   JIA-NING
> Don't be silly!

*Guo-Lun sits and thinks. He absent-mindedly picks up a roll off the table and
starts to eat it.*

The Owner of the noodle stand walks over to a contemplative Guo-Lun.

OWNER
Here's your Stinky Tofu.

INTERIOR. OFFICE HALLWAY. EVENING.

Jia-Chien walks down the now nearly empty corridors.

JIA-CHIEN
Bye.

SECRETARY
Bye.

When she reaches the elevator, she sees Li-Kai sitting asleep on a chair in the lobby. She stares at him, then realizes that the Secretary has been watching her watch him.

SECRETARY
He's got jet lag! Just flew in from Paris! Came right to work! Cute, eh?

The elevator door opens and Jia-Chien is relieved to get into it.

We see Li-Kai's eyelids open slightly, following her.

INTERIOR. JIA-JEN'S ROOM. NIGHT.

Jia-Jen sits at her desk, grading papers. A cat in heat huskily howls from the rooftop. Jia-Jen looks up, thoroughly distracted.

INTERIOR. MR. CHU'S ROOM. NIGHT.

Mr. Chu thumbs through an old recipe book. A pile of well-worn volumes is at his elbow. He writes carefully into a small notebook. He serenely disregards the cat's howling.

MR. CHU
A great teacher said the best way to increase sexual dynamism is to prepare 3 ounces of ginseng, 8 ounces of dried sea cucumber . . .

INTERIOR. JIA-JEN'S ROOM. CONTINUED.

Jia-Jen kneels on her desk, yelling out the window, trying to scare away the cat as Jia-Chien enters.

JIA-CHIEN
What are you doing?

JIA-JEN

That cat's driving me crazy!

Jia-Chien is at the closet replacing underwear.

JIA-CHIEN

At least someone's having some fun around here! *(finding some of her own underwear in the closet)* Ah, here they are—no wonder I couldn't find them.

Jia-Chien looks back up to find Jia-Jen looking at her, a bit flustered.

JIA-CHIEN

I'm sorry about that crack . . . I'm sure you'll find someone—

JIA-JEN

Oh please! Why does everyone think I'm looking for a boyfriend?—I already found someone, thank you!

JIA-CHIEN

(trying to be sisterly)

Jia-Jen, that was what? Nine years ago already. You can't still be heartbroken—

JIA-JEN

It's none of your business!

Jia-Chien scoops up her underwear and walks out.

JIA-CHIEN

Fine!

EXTERIOR. ROAD TO CHU'S. DAY.

Mr. Chu is looking very happy as he takes Shan-Shan home from school.

MR. CHU

We've agreed then. Every day, I'll make you a lunch box.

SHAN-SHAN

But sometimes Mama makes me a lunch box. Then what?

MR. CHU

We'll trade. You give yours to me, that way your mother won't know about it.

SHAN-SHAN

Can you make one for Chen Pei-Hsin too? She's my best friend. She has to buy hamburgers as often as I do.

> MR. CHU

No problem. It's one job and there's enough.

> SHAN-SHAN

Thank you, Mr. Chu!

The two of them enter the alleyway.

INTERIOR. OFFICE. EVENING.

Jia-Chien is gathering her papers to take home at the end of the day, and is surprised to look up to see the Chief standing in the doorway watching her.

> JIA-CHIEN

Chief!

> CHIEF
> *(looking around)*

Hmmm. Your plant is dying.

> JIA-CHIEN

I always forget to water it.

The Chief picks it up and throws it into a trash can.

> CHIEF

You won't be able to take it with you anyhow.

> JIA-CHIEN

I'm fired?

> CHIEF

Don't be ridiculous! It's a little premature to tell you this—I still need approval of the board—but I've put you in to take over the Amsterdam office, vice-president, all our operations over there.

> JIA-CHIEN

Chief, I . . .

> CHIEF

Frankly, you're too young and too good-looking for the job. But all the men I've sent over are idiots, so you'll have to do.

> JIA-CHIEN

But . . .

> CHIEF

But what? C'mon—everyone is angling for this job. What're you waiting for?

JIA-CHIEN

You know I've just bought an apartment here, and—

CHIEF

Rent it out! You'll probably make a profit! *(walking out the door)*
Then again, don't do anything until the board confirms your
appointment.

INTERIOR. IN FRONT OF RAYMOND'S DOOR. NIGHT.

*Raymond opens the door to find Jia-Chien, juggling a few bags of fresh
groceries. He seems a bit surprised, but happy.*

JIA-CHIEN

I felt like cooking!

RAYMOND

My kitchen is at your command!

INTERIOR. RAYMOND'S KITCHEN. NIGHT.

Close on a delicious spread of food being prepared.

*Jia-Chien cooks for Raymond in one of his dress shirts. He sits at the table and
marvels at her skill as more and more dishes appear.*

JIA-CHIEN
(presenting another plate)

This is tsu-an-tofu. Unfortunately, you didn't have a bamboo steamer, but . . . taste it anyway.

RAYMOND

Where's the tofu?

JIA-CHIEN

The tofu is blended in with the chicken. And then it's steamed in the pot until it looks like a bee hive. You then cut it into pieces which you stew with ham in an old hen broth.

RAYMOND

I know I was good, but you really don't have to reward me like this.

JIA-CHIEN

I like cooking elaborate dishes. I wish I could do it at home.

RAYMOND

Do you mean you can't cook tofu at home?

JIA-CHIEN

No, I can't cook at home.

RAYMOND

Doesn't your dad have a big kitchen?

JIA-CHIEN

Yes, but it's off limits to me. If I were to cook there, he'd stop me—I'd be stealing his thunder.

She continues to bring over more food to the table.

JIA-CHIEN

Now try the carp with garlic sauce—it's the very first dish Uncle Wen taught me. And this is Duck Oil Sautéed Pea Sprout. One duck, which makes two dishes with two flavors. A perfect balance of heating and cooling elements in this dish. It's ancient philosophy. Food balanced with energy, flavor, and nature.

RAYMOND

Like mixing ying and yang.

JIA-CHIEN

Take your time. There's also a tofu dumpling coming up.

RAYMOND
You've made enough for ten people!

JIA-CHIEN
(smiling)
I always cook for too many people—it's because I learned how to cook in the huge kitchen of a big restaurant . . . *(another smile)* That kitchen . . .

RAYMOND
What?

She inhales deeply the scent of a dish.

JIA-CHIEN
It's strange—I don't have any childhood memories at all unless I cook them into existence. . . . My memory's in my nose.

RAYMOND
(eating)
I'm terrible with childhood memories—hardly remember a thing.

JIA-CHIEN
You wouldn't believe me if I told you how wonderful and funny and warm my father was in those days. In the afternoons after school, before the dinner rush, he used to bake me bracelets made of bread— *(wiggling her fingers)* I had rings of dough painted with spices and sugar diamonds. He used to let me play around so much in that big kitchen! Jia-Jen was so jealous!

RAYMOND

Here, I'll put this squid around your finger and then nibble it off.

JIA-CHIEN
(annoyed)

Don't play.

RAYMOND

How about I wear it as an earring—

JIA-CHIEN

Getting up to clear a plate
Enough! I'm sorry I got so sentimental tonight.

RAYMOND

Leaning back, not really paying attention to her mood, lighting a cigarette.
Boy, am I stuffed!

She looks back at him, vaguely dissatisfied, while tossing the leftovers into a plastic container.

INTERIOR. RESTAURANT KITCHEN. EVENING.

Close on a huge wok sizzling with delicious food.

Mr. Chu and Old Wen at work, enjoying their jobs and each other's company.

OLD WEN

This smells good.

Mr. Chu presents a plate to Old Wen.

MR. CHU

How is it? Spicy? Say something!

Old Wen makes a face.

MR. CHU

Don't make faces. Say something!

Suddenly—whoosh—Old Wen falls to the floor.

MR. CHU

Old Wen! Old Wen! Old Wen!

INTERIOR/EXTERIOR. AMBULANCE. EVENING.

Mr. Chu holds Old Wen's hand as he is rushed to the hospital.

INTERIOR. HOSPITAL HALLWAY. EARLY MORNING.

Jia-Chien enters and sees her father struggling at the reception desk with complicated hospital forms.

> NURSE
>
> Name. Address. Social Security Number. Family status. Relatives. If he needs special nursing care, please fill out this bottom section.

> JIA-CHIEN
>
> Dad.

> MR. CHU
>
> You're here. It's okay now. They ran some tests in the emergency room, and he feels better now.

> JIA-CHIEN
>
> Was it a heart attack?

> MR. CHU
>
> We'll have to wait for more examinations. Do you have a pen?

> JIA-CHIEN
>
> Let me fill it out.

INTERIOR. HOSPITAL ROOM. NIGHT.

Jia-Chien and Mr. Chu enter the room, as Old Wen begins a wheezy laugh.

> JIA-CHIEN
>
> Uncle Wen.

> OLD WEN
>
> Jia-Chien. Just like me to practically be killed by—a fart! Ha! Blame your father's cooking, it gets worse every week!

> MR. CHU
>
> It's just that you eat too much of it!

> OLD WEN
>
> Come on, give Old Wen a hug. *(she kisses him)* Why'd you grow up to be so pretty?

JIA-CHIEN
(ironic)

To be harassed by men.

OLD WEN

It seems like only yesterday you were a little girl following me around the kitchen. How quickly you learned everything! What a talent, eh Chu?

MR. CHU
(uncomfortable)

Yes, of course.

JIA-CHIEN
(to her father)
Until you banished me from the kitchen.

MR. CHU

Until you learned to do something serious with your life!

JIA-CHIEN

You know you just couldn't conceive of a woman being a real chef!

OLD WEN

Don't start again, you two. *(speaking softly to Jia-Chien, taking her hand, as Mr. Chu walks over to a window)* Yes, you could have become one of the greats. But your father was right to encourage you in your studies. And you, such a success! You owe it all to your father for throwing you out of our smelly old kitchen and keeping you on the right path!

JIA-CHIEN

No one asked me if I wanted such a favor!

OLD WEN

Don't hold a grudge against your father. He's as old and confused as I am. But he's more proud of you than of anything else in the world. I know! Just look at all the feeling and emotion he keeps bottled up inside him. Someday he'll have to express himself to you—or he'll end up in here with something worse than an upset stomach!

They both look over across the room at Mr. Chu, who appears to be pathetically fumbling with the buttons on his sweater, cold and old, unaware that they are talking of him.

Jia-Chien has a sad look on her face.

EXTERIOR. LIANG'S APARTMENT HOUSE. DAY.

The taxi pulls up. Jin-Rong pays, Mrs. Liang gets out.

> MRS. LIANG
> Why didn't you get change? There were ten yuan more!

Mrs. Liang has a Shanghainese accent.

> JIN-RONG
> *(carrying luggage)*
> He was nice enough to take us through that traffic jam in the pouring rain.

> MRS. LIANG
> The meter's still running in a traffic jam! If there's money to be made, they'll make it! Hey, tell him to get out and help with the luggage!

INTERIOR. LIANG'S APARTMENT HOUSE. DAY.

Shan-Shan, Jin-Rong, and Mrs. Liang carry luggage up the staircase.

> MRS. LIANG
> *(angry)*
> They're supposed to carry the luggage for tips! You're just like your sister. You throw out tips like water. But how much does your sister make in a month? How much do you make?

JIN-RONG

Enough!

MRS. LIANG

You're alone. You've got to save all you can! Otherwise who're you gonna depend on when you get old?

JIN-RONG

I'll be depending on whoever you're depending on!

MRS. LIANG
(shocked)

What—no elevator?

Jin-Rong uses her head to gesture them forward.

Mrs. Liang looks bitterly at her daughter, carrying the luggage ahead of her.

INTERIOR. FAST FOOD RESTAURANT. DAY.

Rachel is putting on her uniform as Jia-Ning prepares to leave.

RACHEL

He hasn't even called or come by in a week.

JIA-NING

Maybe he's busy with exams. And . . . I thought you really didn't care for him that much anyway . . . You'd split up with him, no?

Rachel stops putting on her uniform, suddenly on the verge of tears.

RACHEL

It's not true—I was just playing hard to get. But you know, I think I really do love him after all. Strange, isn't it. Why did he stop calling? What should I do now?

Jia-Ning looks uncomfortable.

INTERIOR. JIA-CHIEN'S OFFICE. LATE DAY.

Li-Kai paces the office, his notebook computer on the ground, as Jia-Chien sits at her computer—it's obvious they've been working together all day.

LI-KAI

You honestly think we can pull that many out of Sydney? Why not Bangkok, or Osaka?

JIA-CHIEN
I showed you the projections yesterday. You have a problem with them?

LI-KAI
Oh, you're right. Sorry.

Sitting down.

LI-KAI
I'm just not used to working with someone who isn't a certifiable idiot.

JIA-CHIEN
(playfully)
Or maybe you're just a little too high on yourself.

LI-KAI
(laughing)
Probably—but you know what I'm talking about. Maybe it's because I occasionally get a flash about just how meaningless all this crap really is. Or maybe I'm just tired.

JIA-CHIEN
You want some tea?

LI-KAI

Holding his hands to his head, comically pretending to be a mind reader.
Scotch . . . I sense a bottle of scotch in the vicinity.

Jia-Chien pauses, smiles a bit, then gets up and closes the door. She then goes over to a filing cabinet and pulls from way back a bottle and two shot glasses.

JIA-CHIEN
(pouring)

How did you know?

LI-KAI

An educated guess . . . I figured you spent so much time in here . . .

JIA-CHIEN

I'm really that much of an old maid?

LI-KAI
(laughing)

No, far from it! You just remind me of when I was a student, some of the smartest were also the wildest—we even used to make our own whiskey in chemistry lab and hide it behind the blackboards—

JIA-CHIEN

So you were a chemist?

LI-KAI

That's what I studied to be. In a prior lifetime.

JIA-CHIEN

How'd you get into this . . . ?

LI-KAI

Business? The airline business?

JIA-CHIEN

Yes.

LI-KAI

The same way you did.

JIA-CHIEN

Well I didn't really plan to be—

LI-KAI

Exactly.

JIA-CHIEN
(thoughtful, raising her glass)

To your health.

INTERIOR. JIA-JEN'S OFFICE. EVENING.

Jia-Jen pours out her old tea and fixes herself a fresh cup. She picks up a light blue envelope.

Puzzled, she looks at her name written on the front and opens it.

(subtitled, in italics)
"You appeared like May sunshine with your rose smile, spreading love and warmth"

Jia-Jen looks up, then over to the door. The sounds of a volleyball tournament waft in. She walks over to the window and looks out over the volleyball field, where Ming-Dao is refereeing a game.

Ming-Dao looks up and sees her. He waves. Then, he steps into the game. He jumps onto the ground on his stomach and, in a gesture half-comic, half unintentionally obscene, manages to hit the ball with his butt. The ball flies over the net, to the amazement of the students, who all laugh and applaud. Ming-Dao stands and takes a rather idiotic bow towards Jia-Jen.

Jia-Jen jumps back from the window. She looks like she's in shock.

EXTERIOR. FAST FOOD RESTAURANT. EVENING.

As Jia-Ning leaves, she sees Guo-Lun across the street.

JIA-NING

Torturing yourself again?

GUO-LUN

Actually, I'm waiting for you.

JIA-NING
(looking thoughtful)

Oh.

INTERIOR. GUO-LUN'S APARTMENT. EVENING.

Guo-Lun opens the door and Jia-Ning follows him inside.

It is the penthouse apartment. The windows all around give it a spacious feeling, but the austere decor and the light-colored porcelain bricks on the floor add up to a feeling of coldness.

Guo-Lun gets Jia-Ning some slippers.

JIA-NING

You live here?

GUO-LUN

I sleep here. No one lives here.

JIA-NING

Your parents?

GUO-LUN

Somewhere in Mainland China or California, looking for real estate to invest in. Every few months they stop in to check up on the apartment and the building. They're busy making money.

JIA-NING

Do they stay in the building?

GUO-LUN

No, the building is full of tenants. My grandmother used to live in one of the apartments. But since her stroke, they put her in a nursing home. *(changing the subject)* Would you like something to drink?

JIA-NING

Some ice water.

She looks around at the tasteful, minimalist apartment as he goes to the kitchen.

She turns to a shelf where there are piled a number of expensive looking cameras, camera bags, flashes, and accessories.

He comes back with the glasses.

GUO-LUN

Ice water.

JIA-NING

It's very quiet here.

GUO-LUN

Do you want to hear some music?

JIA-NING

No.

Guo-Lun glances at Jia-Ning. She gets up and walks over to the shelf where the camera equipment is piled up.

JIA-NING

Yours?

GUO-LUN

Yeah.

JIA-NING

I didn't know you were into photography so seriously.

GUO-LUN

I'm not really. Actually, I only take photographs of my grandmother. I visit her every week. The camera just seems to be the only thing she responds to . . . you know, with her eyes . . . It's probably just the flash!

JIA-NING
She can't talk? *(he shakes his head no)* Maybe she doesn't want to be photographed.

GUO-LUN
At first I had the same thought . . . but . . .

INTERIOR. GUO-LUN'S DARKROOM. EVENING.

In the shadows of the red darkroom light, Guo-Lun fixes a picture as Jia-Ning looks on.

GUO-LUN
Look—here she comes.

He points to the photograph, slowly emerging in the chemical bath. It's an extreme close-up, shallow focus of an old, thinning woman's face, with deep-set painful eyes.

Silence. The two of them look down at the photo. Jia-Ning takes Guo-Lun's hand.

EXTERIOR. HIGH SCHOOL GATE. DAY.

Jia-Jen is standing as usual waiting for the bus. She's nervously glancing here and there.

Students are riding out on their motorbikes. Finally, she sees Ming-Dao on his bike coming out. Jia-Jen's heart is beating rapidly, thinking that he'll ride over, but he doesn't see her. He turns down another street and rides away. Her excited face gives way to a blank expression.

EXTERIOR. HALF-CONSTRUCTED APARTMENT BUILDING. EVENING.

We see Raymond's car pull up, and Jia-Chien and Raymond get out and walk in front of the building. There is a police railing across the front door—the building looks abandoned and half-finished.

JIA-CHIEN
This is it. I'm on the tenth floor. Looking out over Taipei.

RAYMOND
(looking around)
Why can't we go in?

                        JIA-CHIEN

It must be dangerous.

An old man walks by and overhears her.

                        OLD MAN

Oh no. Big fraud. Police shut it down.

                        JIA-CHIEN

What do you mean?

                        OLD MAN

This land—it's one big toxic waste dump! *(sniffs)* You smell it? Poison!

                        JIA-CHIEN

I don't smell a thing!

                        OLD MAN
                     (shuffling off)

Hope you weren't one of the suckers who bought into it—company's bankrupt!

Jia-Chien looks at Raymond with a hint of panic in her eyes. The barest hint of a smile plays on his lips.

INTERIOR/EXTERIOR. RAYMOND'S CAR. EVENING.

Raymond pulls up in front of the hospital. He turns to Jia-Chien and lightly touches her arm as she readies to get out of the car.

                        RAYMOND

Hey—I told you you should have invested in art.

She smiles painfully.

                        RAYMOND

Sorry. Bad joke.

Just as Jia-Chien opens the car door, he grabs her shoulder.

                        RAYMOND

Just wanted to cheer you up. If you don't want to stay at home, I'll help you to find a house.

She gets out of the car. He calls to her.

                        RAYMOND

You sure you gonna be all right?

JIA-CHIEN

Of course. Strangely, I feel lighter—freer.

RAYMOND

Like you could fly off to Amsterdam and forget the whole thing!

JIA-CHIEN
(a little wave good-bye)

Exactly.

INTERIOR. HOSPITAL. EVENING.

Jia-Chien walks out of Old Wen's room, which is now empty. She speaks to a passing Nurse.

JIA-CHIEN

Excuse me, May I ask you about Room 22? Mr. Wen?

NURSE

Well, he walked out of here this morning—against the advice of his doctor, too. He is your—

JIA-CHIEN

He's an associate of my father.

She walks down the hall and through a pair of double doors.

INTERIOR. HOSPITAL HALLWAY. EVENING. CONTINUED.

Jia-Chien, a bit lost, asks a Nurse.

JIA-CHIEN

Excuse me, which way is the elevator?

NURSE

Straight down and turn left.

JIA-CHIEN

Thank you.

As she continues down the hall, she is suddenly taken aback—for down the hall, wearing a hospital gown, Mr. Chu, her father, is being led by a Nurse into an examination room. She calls out, but for some reason stops herself short.

She sees another Nurse wheel some fancy looking heart machine into the room her father just went into.

NURSE

This way.

Another Nurse rushes in.

Dissolve:

INTERIOR. HALLWAY. LATER.

Jia-Chien, half hidden behind some equipment, watches the door to the room. Her father comes out, followed by a solemn looking Doctor. They shake hands somberly, as the Doctor gives Mr. Chu a folder—he remarks on some of the papers inside, pointing at them as he explains a last detail to Mr. Chu.

As she begins to approach her father, she is distracted by an old Patient with many tubes and an oxygen mask who is being quickly carried to the Intensive Care Unit.

NURSE

Excuse me.

She then walks to the now empty room where her father was, and looks in where she sees an array of medical instruments, an old woman Orderly cleaning up, and an old Man taking his shirt off.

A Nurse notices that she's staring into the room.

                              JIA-CHIEN
Excuse me.

                              NURSE
May I help you?

                              JIA-CHIEN
What department is this?

                              NURSE
Cardiovascular.

                              JIA-CHIEN
Thank you.

Jia-Chien gets out of the room and anxiously looks again for her father. She sees him entering the elevator at the end of the hall, as the door closes behind him. Alone, she stares at the elevator door, frustrated and confused.

EXTERIOR./INTERIOR. CHU HOUSE. MORNING.

Mr. Chu walks into the house from outside.

INTERIOR. JIA-NING'S BEDROOM. MORNING.

Mr. Chu, wearing his jogging outfit, knocks. The morning wake-up ritual.

                              MR. CHU
Jia-Ning! Jia-Ning! Wake up, sleepy head.

As he walks away, she rolls over, looking a bit ashen and pale.

INTERIOR. JIA-CHIEN'S ROOM. MORNING.

Mr. Chu knocks and opens her door.

She is lying awake in bed, and looks carefully at him.

                              MR. CHU
Good morning.

                              JIA-CHIEN
Good morning, Dad.

He senses she might have something to say to him, and pauses, but then turns and goes out.

INTERIOR. CHU KITCHEN. DAY.

Mr. Chu is preparing Sunday dinner again. He takes a live fish out of the bucket and places it on the counter. Just as he is about to gut it, he steps back and watches it writhe for a moment.

INTERIOR. CHU DINING ROOM. EVENING.

Close on the table brimming over with food.

Cut To:

The meal in progress with the three daughters and Mr. Chu quietly eating.

Mr. Chu puts some food on Jia-Ning's plate. She's hardly eating.

> JIA-NING
>
> Thank you, Dad.

More eating.

> JIA-NING
>
> Dad forgot to put shrimp paste in the flat mushroom.

> JIA-JEN
>
> Shhh . . .

> JIA-JEN
>
> Mrs. Liang has already been back for a few days. Every day, over and over again, she tells Jin-Rong about what happened while she was in America. She's driving Jin-Rong crazy.

> JIA-NING
>
> Shan-Shan said Mrs. Liang's cooking is worse than her mother's.

Jia-Jen and Jia-Ning laugh at this. They notice that Jia-Chien isn't laughing.

> JIA-CHIEN
>
> I have a little announcement, it's about my job. Recently, my company—

> MR. CHU
>
> We read about your apartment fraud in the newspaper.

> JIA-NING
>
> What are you going to do? Will you get your money back?

> JIA-JEN
>
> Did you put all of your savings in that apartment?

Mr. Chu glances down at Jia-Chien, who averts her gaze.

MR. CHU

Of course, you may continue to live here.

He puts some meat on her plate, which she doesn't notice.

INTERIOR. JIA-NING'S ROOM. EVENING.

Jia-Jen enters with a pile of underwear, which she exchanges for another pile from Jia-Ning.

JIA-JEN

Here, these were in my drawers.

JIA-NING

And here's yours. It's getting worse and worse—he should just let us sort our own laundry.

JIA-JEN

He's preoccupied.

JIA-NING

Senile! When would I ever wear one of your big puffed-out blouses—

JIA-JEN

Oh, I'm sorry my wardrobe is so offensive to you!

JIA-NING

You know what I mean.

JIA-JEN

I'm afraid I don't!

INTERIOR. CHU KITCHEN. EVENING.

As Mr. Chu is at the sink doing the dishes, Jia-Chien walks in with more plates from the dining room, eyeing him carefully. As he finishes, he wipes his brow.

JIA-CHIEN

Father, are you ok?

MR. CHU

Yes, of course. Why do you ask?

JIA-CHIEN

Uh, well, you just—

She makes the gesture of him wiping his brow.

MR. CHU
(defensive)
What? You think I don't look well?

JIA-CHIEN
No . . .

The doorbell rings.

MR. CHU
Hmpf! I'm fine!

He leaves the kitchen as she stands there thinking.

EXTERIOR. OUTSIDE OF CHU HOUSE. EVENING.

Mr. Chu walks outside in the rain and opens the door. Jin-Rong, Shan-Shan, and Mrs. Liang enter.

SHAN-SHAN
Mr. Chu!

JIN-RONG
Mr. Chu!

MR. CHU
Shan-Shan! Jin-Rong! Come in, come in!

MRS. LIANG
Oh, Mr. Chu, I should have come by sooner to thank you. But of course Jin-Rong hasn't had the time to bring me over—I practically had to kick her to get her to introduce me. I heard so many times from her about how you've looked out for them, I thought I should come over and thank you personally.

MR. CHU
I've only been doing my duty. Jia-Jen and your older daughter Jin-Feng were old classmates. When they studied in Taiwan, you looked out for her. Now that Jin-Rong is in Taipei alone, and living so close by, it's easy.

INTERIOR. CHU'S LIVING ROOM. EVENING.

Jia-Jen and Jia-Ning enter as everyone is walking through the front door.

SHAN-SHAN
Little aunt, let's paint!

JIA-NING

Just a second.

JIN-RONG

This is for Mr. Chu.

JIA-JEN

You shouldn't have.

MRS. LIANG

Jia-Jen, it's been so long since I've seen you!

JIA-JEN

Mrs. Liang!

MRS. LIANG

Teaching at the same school still?

JIA-JEN

Yes.

MRS. LIANG

Still not married?

JIA-JEN

. . . No.

MRS. LIANG

Ah . . . frankly, marriage isn't all that interesting. If you don't have a good one, it's just a burden you have to drag around and in the end it's best to get a divorce—especially if you're insane enough to marry a real loser like Jin-Rong did.

JIN-RONG

Mother!

Jia-Jen and Jin-Rong trade glances.

MRS. LIANG

And if you don't get a divorce, the thing goes on and on like a tired dog dragging some broken cart and then eventually one party passes away and you're left with yourself . . . Isn't that how it is, Mr. Chu?

MR. CHU

. . . Of course.

JIN-RONG

Ma, what did you say that for?

MRS. LIANG
But it's the truth!

MR. CHU
Why don't you wash some fruit for us, Jia-Jen?

JIA-JEN
Okay.

JIN-RONG
Let me help.

They go to the kitchen.

MRS. LIANG
(noticing Jia-Ning)
Is that your second daughter?

MR. CHU
She's the youngest!

JIA-NING
Nice to meet you, Mrs. Liang.

MRS. LIANG
Nice. And how old are you?

JIA-NING
Twenty.

MRS. LIANG
Ah! You ought to be looking for someone. Don't wait too long like your
big sister. Let's sit down.

Jia-Ning smiles awkwardly.

JIA-NING
Let me make some tea.

SHAN-SHAN
Can we go drawing now?

JIA-NING
All right.

She exits as Jia-Chien enters.

JIA-CHIEN
Mrs. Liang!

MRS. LIANG

You are—

JIA-CHIEN

Jia Chien.

MRS. LIANG

Uh Huh! Right! You're number two. And aren't you pretty!

JIA-CHIEN

Thank you. How are you liking Taipei?

MRS. LIANG

It's okay. Good to be at home. Do you have a boyfriend?

Jia-Chien laughs nervously.

MRS. LIANG

I'm sure you have many. But open your eyes up when you choose. Whatever you do, don't listen to what men say, but watch what they do. Isn't it true, Mr. Chu?

Cut To:

Mr. Chu and Mrs. Liang sitting alone in the living room, talking.

MRS. LIANG

Your daughters aren't bad!

MR. CHU

Your daughters are fine, too.

MRS. LIANG

Mine are no good! The oldest in the middle of this nasty divorce—so sordid, *(leaning in)* I can't even mention to you the details! And my youngest hitched up with a white guy who plays an electric guitar in his garage all weekend—a disaster! He eats hamburgers with onions every day. And when I tried to cook fried rice, the smoke alarm would go off. I'd rather die than live there! Thank God she'll probably be getting a divorce soon too!

Mr. Chu is nodding and smiling politely throughout all this. Mrs. Liang pulls out a pack of cigarettes.

MRS. LIANG

Mr. Chu, I'm sure you don't mind.

MR. CHU
(doing his best to lie)

Of course not. Please.

He fumbles with her matches to light her cigarette.

Cut To:

Chu Hallway, where the three Chu sisters stand back and watch in disbelief.

JIA-CHIEN

What a witch!

The three of them look at each other.

INTERIOR. TECHNICAL HIGH SCHOOL TEACHER'S OFFICE. DAY.

Jia-Jen has received another blue letter.

As before it contains more flowery praise.

(subtitled in italics:)
> *"A breeze blows in, fluttering through your clothes, across your smile.
> In a dreamy garret, I am keeping my late autumn love for you."*

Jia-Jen is even more agitated by this letter. She looks around at the four male teachers in the office. They're all around forty or fifty, reading the paper, drinking tea and wearing reading glasses. One after the other she studies their "late autumn" faces but none seem capable of writing the letter. Jia-Jen grows irritated.

JIA-JEN

"Late autumn love . . ."

INTERIOR. TECHNICAL HIGH SCHOOL CLASSROOM.

As Jia-Jen daydreams by a window, her Students take out their cheat notes during a test.

INTERIOR. TEACHERS' PARTY. DAY.

The teachers' party is taking place in the staff meeting room. They're singing along with the karaoke.

Jia-Jen is late. As she hurries along the corridor, she can hear Ming-Dao singing. The song is Chou Hua Jian's hit "Let me be happy, let me be sad":

MING-DAO
(singing)
So many times, I want to say I love you
So often, I want to say I'm sorry,
You cried, "This is fate. It's over, over."
But give me just one moment, one more look,
Don't take everything away,
Another chance, a little tenderness . . .

It's as if Jia-Jen has received an electric shock. She approaches the stage in a trance.

MING-DAO
(singing)
Don't let me hurt so bad,
You can make me happy, make me sad,
Make me willing to give you everything.

Ming-Dao finishes the song—he has a great voice but mugs it up pathetically. Still, the applause is like thunder. The master of ceremonies asks Ming-Dao to pick someone to sing next.

MING-DAO

Thank you. Thank you. Thank you. I just recently took the job at this school. I'm not that familiar with anyone, but I'd like to hand the mike to Teacher Chu—

Jia-Jen is startled. Everyone is clapping. She doesn't know what to do. As Ming-Dao hands her the microphone, he nearly falls off the stage . . .

JIA-JEN

Be careful.

DISC JOCKEY

Teacher, what do you want to sing?

JIA-JEN

I don't need music, I can sing alone. I'll sing, "Love's Commandments."

(singing)
Love is forever, patient, and kind.
Love isn't jealous, boastful, or crazy
Love doesn't do shameful things—

Jia-Jen's soprano carries through the whole room. Occasionally when she hits the high notes, the mike goes haywire and lets out a piercing, trembling buzz.

The letter flutters in her notebook.

EXTERIOR. SCHOOL GATES. DAY.

As Jia-Jen walks out, Ming-Dao comes by on his motorcycle.

MING-DAO

Wow! The soprano! You're really a good singer!

JIA-JEN

So are you.

Jia-Jen looks at Ming-Dao expecting him to say something more.

MING-DAO

Oh, right, there's something I wanted to ask you! This Sunday, are you free?

Jia-Jen thinks this is it—he's asking for a date.

MING-DAO

I want to take the volleyball team and the girls from the Home Economics Department on an outing. Do you want to come?

JIA-JEN
(disappointed)

An outing?

MING-DAO

You really ought to exercise more. Get some sun! If you've got nothing to do, come with us! Think about it, tell me later! Bye!

Ming-Dao as before smoothly turns the motorcycle and zooms off.

Jia-Jen's certainty about him gives way to confusion.

INTERIOR. PUBLIC BUS. DAY.

The bus is crowded. Jia-Ning sees a pregnant woman get on and stand near her. She gets up and gives her her seat.

INTERIOR. ELEMENTARY SCHOOL CLASSROOM. DAY.

Many students are gathered around Shan-Shan's desk.

> SHAN-SHAN
> Don't crowd me! Don't crowd me! One at a time! Now what do you want?

> STUDENT #1
> Curried beef and rice!

> SHAN-SHAN
> What about you?

> STUDENT #2
> Fried rice.

SHAN-SHAN

Ugh! That's too easy, Mr. Chu won't make that! Order something more difficult.

EXTERIOR. SCHOOL GATE. DAY.

Shan-Shan and Mr. Chu are exchanging lunch boxes.

SHAN-SHAN

Mom's lunch box . . . and tomorrow's menu. G'bye!

INTERIOR. CHU FAMILY'S DINING ROOM. DAY.

Mr. Chu opens the lunch box that Jin-Rong has put together. There's wilted vegetables and hard ribs inside. Mr. Chu chews as if he's eating wax, but otherwise his face is expressionless.

INTERIOR. JIA-CHIEN'S OFFICE. DAY.

Jia-Chien is at her desk, typing at her computer, while Li-Kai lies on the floor, typing at his notebook computer.

JIA-CHIEN

(without looking up from the screen, as she types)

You were right—the Sydney route's gotta be worth half as much as they're asking. To think that the Chief was going to offer $30 million! I bet . . . *(she notices that he's not listening—but rather he's punching away furiously at his computer)*

She stands up to look down at his screen—where she sees that he's in the middle of some computer game.

> LI-KAI
> *(caught in the act)*

What?!

> JIA-CHIEN
> *(laughing)*

So this is what the chief pays you all that money to do—no wonder you're so tired all the time!

> LI-KAI

You should try it—I've already killed 2000 aliens and have saved the world from nuclear destruction—what have you accomplished so far this morning?

> JIA-CHIEN
> *(sitting on the floor beside him)*

Just the beginnings of a small headache. *(looking at screen)* Now how could you kill those aliens, they're so cute.

As Li-Kai laughs, the Chief's Son comes to the door, but stops short when he sees them.

> CHIEF'S SON
> *(flustered)*

I remember now. Forget it.

He turns and walks out. Jia-Chien and Li-Kai trade glances.

> LI-KAI
> *(getting up)*

Hey, do you have a little time right now—I need your help with something. *(offering his hand to help her up)*

> JIA-CHIEN

Sure, I guess.

INTERIOR. TOY STORE. DAY.

Jia-Chien and Li-Kai wander the aisles.

All the toys and clothing have English wording and characters on them.

> LI-KAI

I keep trying to find something Chinese to take back to him, but look at all this.

JIA-CHIEN
He's interested in Chinese culture?

LI-KAI
I wish. I can't believe it's happening so fast, but my son is growing up to be an American. Sometimes I look at him and think he's from another planet—but America is where we live, and that's the way his mother wants to raise him.

JIA-CHIEN
His mother? How does she hold up when you're away?

LI-KAI
She's glad I'm not around. I think the only reason we haven't gotten divorced is that we're both too busy! That sounds so cynical, doesn't it?

JIA-CHIEN
I often find myself sounding just as cynical when it comes to my own personal life. *(picking up a model airplane)* Sometimes I wish I could just—

LI-KAI
—Just pick up and fly away? Sounds like that's what you might be doing pretty soon. I once thought that was the answer, too. Yeah, I remember how I felt right after I graduated Chen-Kong University—

JIA-CHIEN
(suddenly interrupting)
You went to Chen-Kong University?

LI-KAI
Yeah, and when I finished, my father had a place for me all prepared in his chemicals business—

JIA-CHIEN
(really flustered now)
—Chemistry?

LI-KAI
Yeah—remember, the whiskey lab? I loved it as a subject to study, but the thought of spending my life here in the family business—my father, my mother, my girlfriend—well, it was a lot of pressure. I guess I didn't have the courage. I just packed up and escaped.

Jia-Chien looks as though she's in a state of shock.

JIA-CHIEN
Then you went to the States?

LI-KAI

It didn't turn out so great, but it was better for everybody in the long run. Hey, you OK?

JIA-CHIEN

Umm *(grabbing a doll off the shelf)*—this looks Chinese! How about this?

LI-KAI

That? That's "Harvey"—another American TV character. You don't know how many of his videos I've suffered through. And that theme song! I could sing it—

JIA-CHIEN

Please don't.

LI-KAI
(taking the doll)
What the hell—I might as well get him something he likes.

He walks up to the register, as Jia-Chien watches him, thinking.

EXTERIOR. IN FRONT OF THE CHU HOUSE. MORNING.

Mr. Chu is leaving the house, holding a paper bag, when Jin-Rong comes up.

JIN-RONG

Mr. Chu! Mr. Chu!

MR. CHU

Ah, Jin-Rong. Is something the matter? *(looking down the street)* That detective. . . . ?

JIN-RONG

No . . . It's just that Shan-Shan is a bit sick today—she won't be going to school.

MR. CHU

Ah. . . . So you . . . ?

JIN-RONG
(laughing)
I began to wonder why Shan-Shan's lunch box was coming back so cleaned out every day! No one ever finished an entire portion of my short ribs before!

MR. CHU

I see . . . I hope you didn't mind.

JIN-RONG

No, of course not. But I was wondering what you've been doing with the lunches I make for her.

MR. CHU

I eat them myself—every day!

JIN-RONG

I'm so embarrassed—you, a cooking national treasure, eating my lunches!

MR. CHU

It gives me great pleasure—and besides, I haven't much in the way of a sense of taste anymore, so it's the feeling that counts.

JIN-RONG
(looking around, readying to leave)

Yes. In any case, please don't let on to Shan-Shan that I know about this—I think she really enjoys having a little secret with you.

Mr. Chu smiles knowingly.

MR. CHU

Yes, I see.

JIN-RONG

Bye.

Jin-Rong smiles back and waves as she walks away.

INTERIOR. FAST FOOD DRESSING ROOM. DAY.

Rachel is sobbing hysterically.

RACHEL

I loved him! I loved him! How could he do this to me?

JIA-NING

You always said you hardly cared for him!

RACHEL

I pretended because my love was so strong! I was scared! And now he's humiliated me! When I saw him, he . . . I don't want to live anymore!

JIA-NING
(disbelieving)

If only I knew. I didn't have a clue that . . . I thought you two . . .

Rachel has suddenly stopped sobbing, and instead has turned a furious, hate-filled gaze at Jia-Ning.

RACHEL
(in a hate-filled whisper)
Chu Jia-Ning. You? You two . . . ?

Jia-Ning is speechless.

INTERIOR. CHU KITCHEN. DAY.

Close on a sizzling frying pan overflowing with succulent meats.

Mr. Chu is finishing preparations for Sunday dinner, as Jia-Ning enters hesitantly.

JIA-NING
Dad, can I help with something?

MR. CHU
No—you can call your sisters to the table.

She pauses, on the verge of saying something.

JIA-NING
Father?

MR. CHU
(not paying attention)
It's fine.

She goes out.

INTERIOR. CHU DINING ROOM. EVENING.

The Sunday dinner ritual.

Eating in silence. We hear the sound of loud karaoke coming from a neighboring house.

JIA-JEN
Can't they stop for once? Such noise!

JIA-CHIEN
We communicate by eating. They communicate by singing karaoke instead. What's wrong with that?

More eating in silence. Then, at once, both Jia-Chien and Jia-Ning speak up. They both pause for the other to continue, then speak again. Then, smiling, Jia-Chien motions to Jia-Ning to speak.

JIA-NING

I have a little announcement . . .

No one really pays any attention—they all continue to eat.

JIA-NING

I know it sounds incredible, but sometimes things happen this way.

JIA-CHIEN

Which class did you fail?

Jia-Ning can't get the words out. She stutters, stutters, stutters, until it all comes out in a flood of words.

JIA-NING

I met a boy—a man—and we've fallen in love—and he lives basically alone in a very big apartment—and we thought we could share because of so much space—he said his parents will like me so I have decided to move out to live with him—but the main reason is . . . I'm having his baby!

Dead shock around the table.

EXTERIOR. CHU FRONT DOOR. EVENING.

Guo-Lun, a suitcase in one hand, shakes Mr. Chu's hand solemnly and then turns and steps into a waiting taxicab with Jia-Ning.

JIA-NING

Bye!

Behind Mr. Chu stand Jia-Jen and Jia-Chien—all three of them stand there dumbly in stunned disbelief.

INTERIOR. PUBLIC BATH HOUSE. DAY.

Mr. Chu lowers himself into the steamy pool of water. It swallows him up as he closes his eyes and relaxes into stillness.

INTERIOR. KITCHEN. NIGHT.

Jia-Chien and Jia-Jen doing the dishes silently.

JIA-CHIEN

That Jia-Ning! I'm still in a state of shock. Do you think Dad's OK? Where'd he go?

JIA-JEN

Probably over to chat with Mrs. Liang. Don't worry about Dad—he's
fine. Go off to Amsterdam—it's the right thing to do.

Jia-Chien stands there looking as though she wants to say something.

JIA-JEN

It is. I mean it.

JIA-CHIEN

Jia-Jen, do you ever think about what might have happened if you had
gone abroad with—with—with what was his name?

JIA-JEN
(troubled by the turn of the conversation)

Li-Kai.

JIA-CHIEN

Yes. Li Kai, after you got your chemistry degrees?

JIA-JEN

Why are you bringing this up?

JIA-CHIEN

Maybe your whole life would be different.

JIA-JEN

What about my life?

JIA-CHIEN

Do you really want to spend your whole life stuck here? What if I were
to tell you that I had—

JIA-JEN
(cutting her off)

Don't tell me anything! This is home—there's nothing wrong with it!

JIA-CHIEN

This is home and there's nothing wrong with it, but it isn't everything!

JIA-JEN
(slamming down a plate)

But this is Dad's everything, and I know him far better than you do! Jia-
Chien, why is it that you feel that you have to meddle in my life? What
gives you the right to tell me what to feel? *(quieter)* Yes—my heart was
broken by Li-Kai—it's true. And you probably think I'm pathetic for
never getting over it—but at least I had a heart to break.

JIA-CHIEN
(hurt, quiet)
And what do you know of my heart?

JIA-JEN
Nothing, because you never thought me worthy of sharing it!

JIA-CHIEN
No, you're wrong! Ever since mother died you thought you had to act like my parent instead of my sister—YOU shut me out.

The two stand across the table from each other. Jia-Jen is gently crying.

JIA-JEN
I thought you hated me.

JIA-CHIEN
(even more quietly)
Never.

A pause. Jia-Jen looks down

JIA-JEN
I broke the plate.

JIA-CHIEN
It's ok.

INTERIOR. JIA-CHIEN'S OFFICE. DAY.

Jia-Chien sits in her chair, overlooking the city. She can't concentrate on her work.

She dials the phone. Grace's answering machine picks up.

GRACE
(voice off)
Hi, if you're Bo-Kong, don't call me anymore. If you're Mom, remind Dad to drink the good tea I brought him. Everyone else, please leave a message after the beep. I'm abroad on vacation, but I'll check the machine, so SPEAK! [beep]

JIA-CHIEN
Grace, hi. Maybe if you get this message you could call? Nothing really urgent, it's just that we haven't gotten a chance to talk in so long, and—

Suddenly, Jia-Chien's office door bursts open, and a gang of Office Workers tumble in.

WORKERS
(various ad lib)
Congratulations on your promotion! It's official!

Jia-Chien holds the phone, not knowing whether to hang up or continue her message.

INTERIOR. CHU'S LIVING ROOM. NIGHT.

Mr. Chu and Mrs. Liang sit together.

MRS. LIANG
My old family home is Changsha in the Hunan Province. After the war, I moved with my husband to Shanghai. You know Shanghai has a girl's high school, Tong De. Our place was in back of the alley there. My husband also liked to cook—but his mouth only brought him bad luck. *(she pulls out a cigarette)* We'd been in Taiwan less than one year when he got stomach cancer and passed away. *(Mr. Chu lights her cigarette)* I also had to fight tooth and nail to bring up my children alone, it's not easy Mr. Chu. And now look at them—as ungrateful and wayward as yours. Their wings grow strong, they take off, and all our hard work comes to nothing!

Mr. Chu merely grumbles his assent.

INTERIOR. BATHHOUSE. DAY.

Mr. Chu lies on the massage table, as a blind masseur pummels him into oblivion. Mr. Chu doesn't look relaxed.

INTERIOR. OFFICE. NIGHT.

Jia-Chien huddles over her computer, as Li-Kai sits on her desk. She finishes typing something in, then sighs.

JIA-CHIEN
That's it.

LI-KAI
I'll have it translated first thing in the morning.

JIA-CHIEN
(leans back in her chair, covering her eyes)
And then you're off for the negotiations?

LI-KAI

In a couple of weeks. I'll probably go back to the states for a few days, then swing through here again, then on to Sydney. I asked the Chief if he could spare you for a few days over there—I'll need you.

JIA-CHIEN

I'm sure you can handle it alone at this point, no?

LI-KAI

Frankly, with your promotion, it's your decision—technically speaking, you're my boss.

JIA-CHIEN
(again leaning back in her chair, closing her eyes tiredly)
Wrong. I'm your boss, period.

Li-Kai swings her chair around, and begins to massage her face.

LI-KAI

Here, boss.

She sighs, feeling his calm touch on her forehead. Suddenly, though, she freezes.

He senses her embarrassment and pulls back, but she takes his hand and gently brings it to her face. They look into each other's eyes.

They kiss. At first tenderly, then with more passion. Li-Kai lifts Jia-Chien from her chair, carrying her with her legs wrapped around him over to the desk. Suddenly, Jia-Chien's attitude changes—she tenses up a bit as Li-Kai kisses her neck and reaches for her clothes.

LI-KAI
(kissing her and with a low voice)
Jia-Chien . . . *(noticing her change)* What is it?

JIA-CHIEN
You really don't know who I am?

LI-KAI

Of course—

JIA-CHIEN
Call me Chu Jia-Chien!

LI-KAI
(kissing her neck)
Whatever you like!

JIA-CHIEN
(demanding)
Call me Chu Jia-Chien, Chu Jia-Chien!

LI-KAI
(questioning, but going along)
Chu Jia-Chien . . . Chu Jia-Chien!

Li-Kai continues to kiss Jia-Chien. She pushes him away with all her might and stands up. A chair is between them.

LI-KAI
(totally confused)
What?

JIA-CHIEN
Have you really so completely erased the memory of my older sister from your head?

LI-KAI
Excuse me? Your older sister?

JIA-CHIEN
That's right! My older sister! Chu Jia-Jen is my older sister! It's only been nine years since your romance with her in college. Her feelings for you are still the same! To the point that she hasn't even married! But you've completely forgotten her!

Jia-Chien's lipstick is spread all over her face and his face. The two of them arguing like this is rather comical.

LI-KAI
Chu Jia-Jen!

JIA-CHIEN
At last you've remembered?

LI-KAI
(shakes his head)
I don't remember, but this name is . . . I have heard it before.

JIA-CHIEN
You've heard it before?

LI-KAI
I can't really think of anyone named that.

JIA-CHIEN
(nodding her head)
What a brute! What for? Feeling embarrassed?

LI-KAI
I think there's a misunderstanding here. If I did remember such a person, it wouldn't matter if it was or wasn't your sister, I'd have no reason to pretend I didn't know her.

The frenzied mood has subsided. The two of them straighten their clothes.

LI-KAI
I need more information.

JIA-CHIEN
She was also in the Chen-Kong University Chemistry Department. She was your classmate! Do you need more information?

LI-KAI
That's not possible. The same class and major . . . There were only a few girls studying Chemistry. What else is special about her?

JIA-CHIEN
She was your girlfriend. She gave you her first kiss. What else special about her! You tell me!

LI-KAI
No, she wasn't my girlfriend! She wasn't even in my class! I remember now! She was in the same department but not the same class. She was always with Jin Feng!

JIA-CHIEN
You know Jin-Feng?

LI-KAI
She was my girlfriend! But we weren't together after that! She ended up dumping me for some American guy. I saw her last year once, in Chicago. Now I remember, she mentioned her good friend, that must have been Chu Jia-Jen . . . Are you all right?

Jia-Chien's head is spinning. She feels worse than if she'd been found out in her own lie.

JIA-CHIEN
You mean, she made it all up—you must be lying!

LI-KAI
Why would I lie? What's with you, anyway?

> JIA-CHIEN
> *(to herself, stunned)*
My God! She made the whole thing up!

EXTERIOR/INTERIOR. RAYMOND'S APARTMENT. NIGHT.

Jia-Chien rings and rings on the doorbell, but there's no answer.

> JIA-CHIEN
> *(to herself)*
Please be home.

The door swings open, but just a crack. We can see Raymond behind the door, standing with his shirt off.

> JIA-CHIEN
Oh Raymond, thank God you're here. I just had the most absurd experience.

A woman's voice can be heard from the room.

> WOMAN
> *(voice off)*
Raymond, who is it?

> RAYMOND
Oh, no one! *(quietly, to Jia-Chien)* Ah, I'm a little . . .

> JIA-CHIEN
> *(crushed)*
Of course, I understand . . .

> RAYMOND
I'll call you tomorrow!

He closes the door.

INTERIOR. RESTAURANT KITCHEN. NIGHT.

Old Wen, walking slowly, enters the kitchen, to the applause of the entire kitchen staff (though Mr. Chu is not there yet).

> ASSISTANTS
Welcome back, Old Wen!

Various ad libs from the staff—"Don't fart near me, please!" etc.

Old Wen is visibly touched by the reception, but mugs it up.

OLD WEN
Back to work you fools! Ach, all this emotion is wearying.

He sits down on a stool and waves away the crowd, which still stands around watching him.

ASSISTANT
Chef Wen . . .

OLD WEN
(closing his eyes)
Just a second!

The room falls uncomfortably silent as the staff watches Old Wen sitting there, with his eyes closed.

Still he sits there.

The Assistant goes up to him, nudges him slightly, then feels for his pulse. He turns quietly to the group.

ASSISTANT
Chef Wen? Chef Wen?

Wide shot:
The sound of bubbling pots, as the stunned group just stands there.

INTERIOR. CHU HOUSEHOLD. NIGHT.

Jia-Chien enters the dark living room. As she walks toward her room, she is startled by her father's silhouette.

JIA-JEN
(noticing something's wrong)

Why are you so late? *(pause)* Uncle Wen is gone.

INTERIOR. BUDDHIST TEMPLE. DAY.

An enormous chamber with walls lined with high cabinets. People mill about, amid incense smoke and religious chanting. The scene is full of color, sound, smoke, voices. Mr. Chu and Jia-Chien walk over to one of the cabinets with a large urn.

JIA-CHIEN

B South 7204. Should be around here . . .

They find the correct cabinet and place the urn inside.

EXTERIOR. BUDDHIST TEMPLE. DAY.

Mr. Chu sits with Jia-Chien in the rain, softly crying. In their grief, Mr. Chu and Jia-Chien seem more together than ever before.

INTERIOR. CHU DINING ROOM. DAY.

Mr. Chu sits despondently as Jia-Chien prepares him tea with an old-fashioned tea set.

She places the tea in front of him.

He picks it up, looks at it, smells it.

> MR. CHU
> I don't want to drink tea. I will drink water.

> JIA-CHIEN
> Drink it. This is your favorite mountain tea. You'll feel better.

> MR. CHU
> My taste has died. I will drink water.

INTERIOR. CHU KITCHEN. DAY.

Jia-Chien goes to the tap and pours water into a plain cup. She looks around at all the canisters and utensils.

EXTERIOR. TAIPEI STREETS. DAY.

Traffic moves by gracefully.

INTERIOR. JIA-JEN'S BEDROOM. DAY.

Jia-Jen sits on her bed, the various love letters spread out around her. Suddenly, the sound of a man and woman singing karaoke comes through her window. She angrily gets up, looks through her window, then grabs a tape and puts in into her tape player. She turns it way up.

The Music Sounds: Hallelujah! Hallelujah!

She pulls out a stick of lipstick.

EXTERIOR. SCHOOL GATE. DAY.

Jia-Jen marches through the gates with her new hair style, sporting some bright new clothes. Some of the students whistle.

Fade out on the Hallelujah music.

INTERIOR. TEACHER'S OFFICE. DAY.

Jia-Jen finds her desk empty; suspiciously she searches around—and finds another envelope.

EXTERIOR. VOLLEYBALL COURT. DUSK.

Jia-Jen looks out and sees the volleyball game going on. It's just before the end of the day; an agitated feeling pervades the school. The Orchestra can be heard practicing. A few students pass by. The student sweeping the corridor raises a cloud of dust. This, added to Jia-Jen's overworked imagination, pushes her close to the breaking point. She wants to stride out to the court and get things straight with Ming Dao, but she can't muster the courage.

The volleyball court is at the center of the school. Near it is a stage where activities and ceremonies involving the whole school take place. Jia-Jen approaches the stage and climbs the stairs. She grabs the microphone and begins yelling through the powerful loudspeakers.

Intercut various students and faculty hearing her on the sound system.

> JIA-JEN
>
> Can a single hand clap alone? Can a ballplayer play without an opponent? Why do I only get to talk to thin air about love? Who's writing those letters? If you have any guts, show yourself to me! Come on! Step up! Who's been putting those disgusting letters on my desk every day? Who? Who dares to write like that and won't admit it? Do you think you can hide from me? That I'll just forget it? Just wait until I put every one of those letters up on the bulletin board and check everyone in this school's handwriting! Then see where you can hide!

After shouting this into the microphone, not only the whole volleyball team stops and looks quietly at her, but everyone in the school.

Seconds later Jia-Jen realizes she's acted like an insane woman.

INTERIOR. JIA-JEN'S CLASSROOM. DUSK.

It's getting dark. A few students are still hanging around.

The Class Leader comes out of the classroom, looking very sorry.

> CLASSMATES
>
> What happened?

> CLASS LEADER
>
> Teacher said she'd forgive us for the letters.

Ming-Dao walks up.

> MING-DAO
>
> You really went too far with that joke!

The students are silent.

INTERIOR. CLASSROOM. DUSK.

Jia-Jen is crying as she erases the chemical equation from the blackboard. She hasn't expected to see Ming-Dao. He enters the room. She turns to face him, overwhelmed with embarrassment.

> MING-DAO
> The outing with the volleyball team is changed to next week. Will you be coming?

Jia-Jen looks surprised.

> MING-DAO
> How about this? I'll sign you up and if it turns out you've got something else at the time, just let me know, okay? (pausing) I'm sorry if those little jerks hurt your feelings.

She sniffles.

She puts her head on his shoulder and sobs quietly. He looks a bit uncomfortable. She looks up at him. Just as he's about to say something, she plants a firm kiss on his lips. He looks completely stunned, but then seems to begin to enjoy it.

INTERIOR. RAYMOND'S ART GALLERY. DAY.

Jia-Chien is pouring her heart out to Raymond, who looks increasingly uncomfortable.

> JIA-CHIEN
> I'm sorry about the other night—it was just a really confusing experience. I didn't know who else to go to but you.

> RAYMOND
> No, I'm sorry.

> JIA-CHIEN
> Why should you be sorry? Of course you have your own life. In any case, I've made some decisions.

> RAYMOND
> I have my own big decision to announce.

He pauses.

> JIA-CHIEN
> Yes?

RAYMOND

You know I don't really like the settled-down life. I'm still a little mixed about it, but overall, I have to say it's been something that, well, you know Sophia? No? I'm sure I've mentioned her a couple of times, nothing really important, until, well—

JIA-CHIEN
(suddenly realizing)

You're getting married!

RAYMOND

I would have told you about it sooner, but it happened so suddenly. She's really changed my life. Maybe she'll change my future. It sounds even more absurd than your story. I didn't know how you'd take it.

JIA-CHIEN
(trying to hide the incredible hurt and confusion)

But—congratulations!

RAYMOND

I knew you'd understand! And I know you'll really like and admire Sophia—she's quite an accomplished painter. She's also managing my gallery—and she's a good cook, too! But, you know, I don't really see this marriage changing so much of my life—she's actually moving into my apartment this weekend. Same place, same job,—really, the same life.

JIA-CHIEN

Of course.

An awkward pause.

RAYMOND
(checking his watch)

Two o'clock already!

JIA-CHIEN

Oh, I'd better be going.

RAYMOND

I can drive you wherever.

JIA-CHIEN

I'm fine.

RAYMOND

Actually, I've got a couple of hours free. Maybe—are we still "good friends"? I mean, I have my office in the back of the gallery, you know . . .

JIA-CHIEN
(on the verge of murdering him, but holding it all in)
Sorry! *(gathers her things quickly)* Got to go!

She's gone.

RAYMOND
(his voice trailing)
See you around, ok?

EXTERIOR. GALLERY. CONTINUED.

Jia-Chien walks a few steps, then throws up into some bushes.

INTERIOR. CHU FAMILY LIVING ROOM. DAY.

A bright ray of light falls through the room. Mr. Chu sits looking very tranquil, as the Manager from the restaurant pleads with him.

MANAGER
Think about it, please! The restaurant really needs you!

MR. CHU
There are many good young chefs. Don't worry, you'll find someone to take over.

MANAGER
But a master chef like you with such a deep understanding and control of the art of Chinese cuisine . . . there are so very few . . . Even if you don't do anything, just standing there, you're a living cookbook, a national treasure!

MR. CHU
How long do you want me to stand in the kitchen? Until heaven knocks me down like Chef Wen? Everyone says "People die for money, Birds die for food." If someone wants to die for money that's their business, but to die for food, that's for the birds! It's not worth it!

MANAGER
That's so, but your whole life is devoted to the art of cooking. What a pity to just let it go.

MR. CHU
People today are so insensitive. There's no sense in cooking exquisite food anymore. After forty years of Chinese food in Taiwan, everything is mixed up. Food from all different provinces mixed up just like rivers running into the sea. It's all one flavor! Even a mess of slop can pass for

"Joy Luck Dragon Phoenix!" What more can I say? Fortunately, I'm not going to waste my whole life on this stuff.

At this moment, Jia-Chien enters the house, looking ill and weak from her encounter with Raymond. The Manager sees her as she walks towards her room.

> MANAGER
> Ah, Miss Chu, please convince your father not to retire!

> JIA-CHIEN
> *(to her father)*
> You're retiring from the restaurant?

He just looks up at her.

> JIA-CHIEN
> *(to the manager, curtly)*
> It's his own business. He does what he wants to do.

She walks to her room.

INTERIOR. JIA-CHIEN'S ROOM. INTERCUT.

As she enters the room, she closes the door behind her, then stands there, thinking . . .

BACK TO THE LIVING ROOM.

The Manager is about to leave. A little smile plays on his lips.

> MANAGER
> Master Chu, you're thinking of opening your own restaurant, aren't you?

Mr. Chu is a little surprised, but shows little response.

> MANAGER
> Be sure to let me know, I'll follow you!

Mr. Chu smiles but doesn't say anything.

INTERIOR. LIANG HOUSE. DAY.

> MRS. LIANG
> I see Mr. Chu worries a lot about his three daughters.

> JIN-RONG
> Isn't that the essence of raising children?

MRS. LIANG
And even harder for a single man to do.

JIN-RONG
It's been so many years. He should be used to it by now.

MRS. LIANG
When did Mrs. Chu die?

JIN-RONG
When Jia-Ning was four years old, about sixteen years ago.

MRS. LIANG
A widower usually has a short life. Why hasn't he thought of marrying
again?

JIN-RONG
Maybe because of his daughters.

MRS. LIANG
Wise up. You end up raising daughters for other people. Only the ones
nobody wants end up hanging around.

JIN-RONG
If that's really what you think, stop haranguing me and Jin-Feng.

MRS. LIANG
What do you think about Mr. Chu?

JIN-RONG

What about him?

MRS. LIANG

I think he is a nice person. He can really cook. He doesn't talk much, but we really connect.

INTERIOR. CHU DINING ROOM. DAY.

Another Sunday dinner, only this time without Jia-Ning.

Now, no one is eating or talking. But Jia-Jen radiates a strange energy. She and Jia-Chien both start talking at once. They pause, then start again.

JIA-JEN

Uh, I have a little announcement.

Mr. Chu leans back in his chair, not knowing what's coming.

JIA-JEN

You see, like Jia-Ning—

JIA-CHIEN

You're pregnant!

JIA-JEN

No! Nonsense! But, well, I—it's like—oh!

She pushes back from the table with startling energy.

JIA-JEN

We just couldn't wait . . . he wanted to . . . but I'm a Christian so . . . The minister married us this morning—hold on! He's waiting right outside! One second!

She runs to the front door and flings it open—so that it slams between Ming-Dao's legs.

JIA-JEN

Come in! Come in! Come in!

MING-DAO
(his usual dumb, painful smile)

Whoa!

She grabs him by the arm and drags him in.

JIA-JEN

Father, Jia-Chien—my husband, Chou Ming-Dao!

                              MING-DAO
   Hi!

Ming-Dao waves meekly at them.

EXTERIOR. CHU HOUSE. DAY.

*Mr. Chu and Jia-Chien stand dumbfounded as Jia-Jen and Ming-Dao, lugging a
back pack, climb onto his moped and, with a honk, a tearful wave from Jia-Jen,
and a skid of tires, they're away!*

INTERIOR. JIA-CHIEN'S ROOM. MORNING.

Mr. Chu knocks on her door lightly, and opens it.

He sees Jia-Chien gently asleep.

He watches her for a moment.

                              MR. CHU
                            (whispering)
   Jia-Chien . . .

She doesn't hear. He sighs.

                              MR. CHU
                             (yelling)
   Jia-Chien!

She awakens with a jolt.

                              JIA-CHIEN
   You scared me!

                              MR. CHU
                           (walking away)
   It's late!

INTERIOR. JIA-JEN'S ROOM. MORNING.

*Mr. Chu has already moved out much of her furniture and has packed boxes up
and stacked them, etc.*

Jia-Chien puts down her briefcase.

                              JIA-CHIEN
   Pa, what are you doing?

MR. CHU

For Jia-Jen, I'm packing her things.

She runs over to help him stack a heavy box.

JIA-CHIEN

Here, let me get that.

MR. CHU

I'm fine.

JIA-CHIEN
(looking around)
I always liked this room when I was a kid.

MR. CHU

It was where your mother sat—when she wanted to be by herself. Mrs. Liang says that this room has plenty of light, nice air, and it would be the perfect place for an exercise bike.

JIA-CHIEN

Mrs. Liang?

MR. CHU

I stopped by Jin Rong's place last night—and talked to them about Jia-Jen's news.

JIA-CHIEN

Dad, I'm late—but I'll be back early from work this evening. Don't move any more until I come back?

INTERIOR. CHU LIVING ROOM. NIGHT.

Mr. Chu sits as Mrs. Liang rattles on again, dragging on a cigarette. Jia-Chien sits a bit apart from them.

MRS. LIANG

Let me tell you something. Kids are creditors who've come to collect for what we've done in the last life. They don't know gratitude, none of them. We'd be better off never having had them. Buddhists say, "Life is a boundless sea of bitterness." Only in turning back to shore do we have any hope of happiness. But instead of turning back, we get married! And marriage is the source of all our trouble and suffering. A series of worry, disappointment, misery, conflict, and ingratitude. Oh! I suddenly remembered why I'm in such a good mood! Jin-Rong's divorce decree came through today. I'm going to have it framed so she'll always remember Mama's advice: ''Don't marry that bastard!'' I'll frame it and put it above the toilet.

Mr. Chu laughs uneasily.

> MRS. LIANG

Stop worrying about those little creditors and start thinking more about yourself.

Jia-Chien looks back and forth between the two old folks.

INTERIOR. CHU HOUSE. DAY.

Ming-Dao is working like a horse, moving boxes across the living room to a waiting minivan outside, as Jia-Jen and Jia-Chien talk.

> JIA-JEN

Be careful! Watch your step! *(grabbing a vase and putting it in her bag)* Dad won't mind if I take this, will he?

> JIA-CHIEN

No. But Mrs. Liang will.

> JIA-JEN

What do you mean?

> JIA-CHIEN

She's been over here almost every night.

> JIA-JEN

You're kidding.

> JIA-CHIEN

In any case, I decided not to go to Amsterdam for now.

Ming-Dao drops a box on his foot.

> MING-DAO

Owww!

> JIA-JEN

You okay? Be careful.

> MING-DAO
> *(picking up the box again)*

No problem!

> JIA-CHIEN

Say, I was surprised you married Ming Dao, given that he's not a Christian.

JIA-JEN
(knowingly—watching him through a window)
Oh . . . He will be . . .

Jia-Chien smiles.

INTERIOR. TEA HOUSE. DAY.

Jia-Chien sits at a table in a beautiful old Japanese-style teahouse, waiting.

She sees Li-Kai enter, and motions him over to her table. She seems a little embarrassed to see him.

WAITRESS
Welcome! One person?

LI-KAI
I'm meeting someone here.

JIA-CHIEN
Thanks so much for coming. I thought you might not show up.

LI-KAI
Why?

JIA-CHIEN
The other night . . .

A Waitress comes to the table.

WAITRESS
Sir, what kind of tea would you like to have?

LI-KAI
(gesturing to the tea things on the table)
You're having?

JIA-CHIEN
Mountain tea.

LI-KAI
Same for me.

WAITRESS
Ok. Thank you.

The Waitress leaves as they sit in silence a moment, uneasy. Jia-Chien prepares the tea.

LI-KAI

You know, I have a feeling I understand what you might have been going through, even if I couldn't really explain it.

JIA-CHIEN

Neither can I . . .

LI-KAI

It's complicated—and I can understand that.

JIA-CHIEN
(feeling more relieved)

Thanks.

She pours the tea.

LI-KAI

By the way, word's out about your turning down the promotion. I must say everyone is surprised—I hope I didn't have anything to do with it.

JIA-CHIEN

Not at all. Well, maybe a tiny bit, but . . . I don't know. It's a whole series of things; a wedding in the family—actually a couple of them— and someone died. A bad investment; all of a sudden everything— whoosh!—gone. Plus my father's health. So I've decided to stay with my father for a while. I think he needs me . . .

LI-KAI

The Chief has asked me to see if or when you'll be changing your mind.
But what the hell. It's just a job.

She pours him some more tea.

LI-KAI

I'm glad, you know?

JIA-CHIEN

Glad?

LI-KAI

That we didn't make love. Not that I still wouldn't want to! But—seeing
you now, like this, I'm actually quite happy.

JIA-CHIEN

Me too.

LI-KAI

Because I really do think we can be good friends.

JIA-CHIEN

Of course we will.

He smiles shyly, then reaches out his hand.

LI-KAI

Then—good friends?

She smiles, offering her hand back to his for a shake.

JIA-CHIEN

Good friends.

They shake hands. Jia-Chien laughs to herself, half-sad, half-happy.

INTERIOR. GUO-LUN'S APARTMENT. DAY.

*Jia-Chien sits with Jia-Ning, chatting. There are some baby toys that Jia-Chien
brought as gifts, unwrapped on the floor around them.*

JIA-CHIEN
(spinning a top)
When you were a baby, I would sit in front of you and spin this for
hours at a time—you wouldn't let me stop!

                    JIA-NING
                    (laughing)
Well please stop now—I'm getting nauseous again!

                    JIA-CHIEN
                    (getting up)
And I should go—I told dad I'd help shop for this weekend's dinner.

                    JIA-NING
Since when does dad send out written invitations? I guess he wants to
make it more formal, to introduce Guo-Lun and Ming-Dao.

                    JIA-CHIEN
He mentioned something to me about making his own little
announcement.

                    JIA-NING
Mrs. Liang!

                    JIA-CHIEN
Probably. But my feeling is that—unlike you and Guo-Lun—they'll take
their time with the engagement, during which I hope he'll realize what
a nightmare she is.

                    JIA-NING
It's just the shock of recent events. It's gone to his head. I never thought
he'd go crazy like this, or else maybe I'd have—

                    JIA-CHIEN
Don't blame yourself—he's not going crazy. He's an old horse.

                    JIA-NING
But horses don't get married.

EXTERIOR. TAIPEI STREETS. DAY.

Ming-Dao and Jia-Jen are zipping through the streets on his motorcycle.

INTERIOR. CHU FAMILY'S KITCHEN. DAY.

*Mr. Chu is absent-minded today. His manner as he cooks isn't his usual steady
one. Sometimes the pots are boiling over, sometimes the gas is completely
extinguished. He seems agitated.*

INTERIOR. GUO-LUN'S APARTMENT. DAY.

Jia-Ning helps Guo-Lun comb his hair.

INTERIOR. CHU FAMILY'S KITCHEN. DAY.

Mr. Chu squeezes the juice from bean curd wrapped in a cheese cloth.

INTERIOR. LIANG'S HOUSE. DAY.

Jin-Rong is braiding Shan-Shan's hair.

Mrs. Liang, obviously very serious about the coming dinner at the Chu's, enters the room with a dark flowered Chi Pao.

> MRS. LIANG
> What do you think? Huh?

Jin-Rong looks uneasily at her mother.

INTERIOR. CHU FAMILY'S KITCHEN. DAY.

Mr. Chu drops some pots while in the midst of his preparations.

EXTERIOR. CHU BACKYARD. DAY.

Ming-Dao and Guo-Lun chase down a couple of terrified chickens in the alley behind the Chu house.

> GUO-LUN
> Over here, Ming Dao!

MING-DAO

OK!

MR. CHU

Don't just run around! One of you chase it, and one of you grab it!

INTERIOR. CHU FAMILY'S KITCHEN. MOMENTS LATER.

Mr. Chu is absorbed by an intricate carving on the side of a watermelon.

GUO-LUN

Ming-Dao! Ming-Dao! This way!

MING-DAO

Coming! Coming!

GUO-LUN

I got it!

Totally distracted by the ruckus he's hearing outside, Mr. Chu slips the knife through the watermelon, destroying the delicate work.

EXTERIOR. CHU HOUSE. EVENING.

Jia-Chien runs out the door to open the gate for Mrs. Liang, Jin-Rong, and Shan-Shan. They come bearing gifts.

JIA-CHIEN

Jin-Rong and Mrs. Liang.

SHAN-SHAN

Mr. Chu!

MRS. LIANG

I brought a bottle of good wine and a tie for your father.

JIA-CHIEN

You really shouldn't have.

MRS. LIANG

I should have been here earlier to help. *(turning to Jin-Rong and pointing to her blouse.)* How is my pin?

JIN-RONG

It's fine.

Mrs. Liang walks ahead inside.

JIN-RONG

Sorry, we're disturbing you.

JIA-CHIEN

Come on, not at all.

INTERIOR. CHU DINING ROOM. NIGHT.

The two families crowd the dining room table. Before them is a formidable feast of at least a dozen courses.

JIA-JEN

In the name of Jesus Christ. Amen.

MR. CHU

Come on, toast.

EVERYBODY

Toast! Toast!

MRS. LIANG

Come on, please help yourselves.

MR. CHU

I didn't prepare much.

MRS. LIANG

Mr. Chu! Too many dishes already! Help yourselves!

MR. CHU

Winter Melon Soup.

Cut To:
The table overflowing with food.

The large group is busy eating and talking, as Mr. Chu goes back and forth from the kitchen.

The meal progresses.

SHAN-SHAN

Today's Red Seven Star Fish was too big. They're best if they're about two pounds.

MRS. LIANG

Listen to yourself! So picky already. If you keep being so picky when you grow up, you'll never find a husband.

Mrs. Liang raises her glass.

MRS. LIANG

You girls have been lucky! Your father's cooking is superb! Look at this wonderful cuisine! Looks good, smells good and tastes good.

MR. CHU

Jia-Jen. You two, bottoms up!

Ming-Dao raises his glass.

He looks sheepishly at Jia-Jen. They drink.

MR. CHU

Jia-Ning. You two, bottoms up!

MRS. LIANG

Don't drink too much!

MR. CHU

I'm fine.

Mrs. Liang smirks.

MR. CHU

Jia-Chien, bottoms up!

Ad libs all around.

Mr. Chu stands and clinks his glass to quiet everyone.

The three daughters look nervous.

MR. CHU

Fate has brought us to this table tonight—

MRS. LIANG

That's right! Although we're not actually all relatives, it's like we're family.

Mr. Chu begins again.

MR. CHU

Well, since we're like one big family, I suppose there's nothing we should hide from each other. And yet, for a long time I have kept something to myself. I didn't want to hide any secrets from you, but I also didn't want to worry you with my personal affairs. Living under the same roof, leading separate lives, we worry for each other. Mutual worry, that's what makes us a family. And . . . if I don't say anything, then nobody gets worried. And if I do say it, it's because I can't hold it in any longer. Life isn't like cooking after all. I can't wait until all the

ingredients are properly prepared and laid out before starting to cook. Anyway, after the first bite, the only thing that counts is the taste.

At this remark, everyone puts down their chopsticks and looks at him. It's clear he's a tiny bit tipsy.

MR. CHU
(sitting down)

Ahh . . . We'll talk some more after we finish dinner!

JIA-CHIEN

Dad, if you have something to say, go ahead.

JIA-NING

I think we know what you're going to say at any rate.

MR. CHU

You do?

JIA-JEN
(to Jia-Chien)

Let Dad say it himself.

MRS. LIANG

Mr. Chu, just say it! Don't wait until the dishes get cold.

He stands again.

MR. CHU

So be it! The situation has come this far. With this house so full of old memories but now so empty of people . . . , I have decided to sell it. I have found a nice place on Kum Dao. It will need some alterations and new wiring and plumbing, but in a few months it will be ready to move into.

Jia-Jen and Jia-Ning look at Jia-Chien. They don't know what to think.

There is a silent pause.

MRS. LIANG

Well, congratulations. It sounds very nice. New people, new house, new life.

MR. CHU

All right. Now, Auntie Liang, I'll make a toast to you. I haven't really been taking care of Jin-Rong and Shan-Shan all that well, but I swear that so long as I, Old Chu, have one breath left, I'll see to it that mother and daughter never go cold or hungry, and that our new home will always be there to welcome your visits.

He pulls out the medical report and hands it to Mrs. Liang.

MR. CHU

This is a complete medical report I had done at the Veteran's Hospital last month. It shows I am in excellent health. I now ask for your daughter's hand. Please, we ask for your approval. Here's to you!

He tosses back his glass of wine.

MING-DAO
(the only one to toast)

All right!

He looks around to see that everyone else is in shock. Mrs. Liang's face turns ash gray.

JIA-JEN

Dad, you're drunk. Don't drink anymore—you're obviously confused.

MR. CHU

I'm not drunk at all. Jin-Rong!

Mr. Chu looks at Jin-Rong, as does everyone else. She bravely raises her head.

JIN-RONG

Mr. Chu and I. . . . We've thought for a long time. But as you all know, with this terrible divorce, we've had to keep our love a secret until now . . . But—he loves all of you and he loves Shan-Shan, and—we have always hoped for your understanding. For me, of course, I want to be with him, at his side.

JIA-JEN
(shell shocked)

Jin-Rong! Please don't say anymore!

JIA-NING

Is there a mistake?

JIA-CHIEN

Dad, are you crazy? You're talking nonsense!

MR. CHU

I'm not crazy. I know exactly what I am saying.

JIN-RONG

Ma? Ma?

Mrs. Liang faints amid a crash of dishes, then almost immediately re-awakens and begins thrashing about in a crazed state. Everyone jumps up and rushes to her aid. Chairs clatter to the ground as the two families attempt to control and help her.

JIN-RONG

Maaa!

MR. CHU
(going to her)
Quick, unbutton her collar!

MRS. LIANG
(slapping him away)
Keep your dirty hands off of me! Goddamn you, Old Chu! How dare you snatch my daughter—

MING-DAO

Here, Guo-Lun, help me carry her to the sofa.

GUO-LUN

Be careful!

MR. CHU

Put her on the sofa!

MRS. LIANG
(struggling as the men carry her)
Damn you! Shame on all of you! Don't touch me. I want to go home. Jin-Rong, come with me. Let me tell you, Old Man, as long as I have my last breath, you'll never touch my daughter again. Shan-Shan, let's go home.

JIN-RONG
Mama, please calm down. Better take her to our house.

Jia-Jen and Jia-Ning crowd around Ming-Dao and Guo-Lun as they carry the screaming Mrs. Liang to the front door. Jin-Rong and Shan-Shan follow.

MRS. LIANG
What kind of world are we living in? I want to die! What kind of family is this? Sin! Sin! You'll pay for this for the next THREE lives!

MR. CHU
(to Jin-Rong, as they exit)
Here, I'll take Shan-Shan! C'mon!

MRS. LIANG
I curse you all. I want to go back to America!

Everyone hustles out.

In a second, the house has become incredibly still.

Only Jia-Chien stands next the dinner table, amid the upturned chairs, broken dishes and glasses, spilled food.

Alone.

EXTERIOR. TAIPEI STREETS. MONTAGE.

A traffic cop stands on a pedestal and directs traffic at a busy intersection.

INTERIOR. CHU KITCHEN. DAY.

A series of shots echoing the opening montage of food preparation and cooking—only this time cut back to reveal Jia-Chien as the chef.

Wide: We see that there are boxes stacked against the walls and that many of the furnishings and wall hangings are already gone.

The phone rings.

JIA-CHIEN

Hello? Guo-Lun, how are you?

INTERCUT WITH GUO-LUN'S APARTMENT.

Jia-Ning sleeps with a tiny baby asleep on her stomach. Guo-Lun is on the cordless phone, whispering as he watches them.

> GUO-LUN
>
> Yes, wonderful! But we've been awake all night. I don't have the heart to wake them.

> JIA-CHIEN
>
> Of course not! You should all sleep with my blessings. And I'll be back here visiting in just a few months in any case.

> GUO-LUN
> *(shy)*
>
> So, good-bye—and let us know all about Amsterdam. And thank you for all your help these past few months.

> JIA-CHIEN
>
> And you take good care of your girls.

> GUO-LUN
>
> Yes. . . . And say hi to Jia-Jen and Ming-Dao for me.

> JIA-CHIEN
>
> Actually, they can't make it tonight, either. *(while talking on the phone, she throws a pile of noodles into a pot of boiling water)* They've got a big day today themselves.

> GUO-LUN
>
> Bye.

> JIA-CHIEN
>
> Bye.

INTERIOR. CHURCH. DAY.

Close on Ming-Dao's head, as a hand pushes it under water.

> MINISTER
>
> Do you believe that the Lord Jesus Christ has forgiven your sins and made you a new person?

> MING-DAO
>
> Yes.

Ming-Dao is happily making bubbles and gurgling as the Minister continues. The Minister looks down, annoyed.

MINISTER

Do you believe in following Jesus Christ all the days of your life and unto eternity?

MING-DAO

Yes.

MINISTER

Believe in your heart. Say yes from your mouth. In the name of the Father, Son and Holy Spirit, I baptize you. Amen.

Ming-Dao pops his head up, smiling and coughing a bit.

The Minister looks even more annoyed. He quickly pushes the surprised Ming-Dao's head back under water.

From the congregation, we see Jia-Jen looking happily on. Two women stand behind her, both in their early thirties. They trade glances with each other as they watch the hunky Ming-Dao stand up out of the water in his wet tee-shirt.

INTERIOR. NEW MR. CHU HOUSE. DAY.

We see Jin-Rong sitting from behind, as Mr. Chu approaches her, his coat in hand.

Jin-Rong stands up, to reveal that she is very pregnant.

Mr. Chu gently kisses her.

MR. CHU

How are you feeling?

JIN-RONG

Fine . . . just a bit exhausted. Why don't you go on ahead . . .

MR. CHU

No problem—I'll pick Shan-Shan up afterwards. You stay here and rest.

As he turns to go, she holds his arm.

JIN-RONG

I love you.

He smiles.

EXTERIOR. STREET IN FRONT OF CHU HOUSE. DAY.

Mr. Chu pulls up in a taxi. He gets out and walks to the front door of the house. There's a "For Sale" sign up, with a big "Sold" sticker across it. He pulls out his keys and is about to enter when he pauses, puts his keys back into his pocket, and rings.

EXTERIOR. CHU HOUSE. EVENING.

Jia-Chien opens the door for Mr. Chu.

> MR. CHU

Hi.

> JIA-CHIEN

Hi. Come in, I'm just finishing up. I'm afraid you're the only one coming—everyone else sends their regards. Where's Jin-Rong and Shan-Shan?

> MR. CHU

Jin-Rong was feeling a bit tired. Shan-Shan is with her grandma.

> JIA-CHIEN

No need to take off your shoes. Just come in. Have you gotten the results of Jin-Rong's ultra-sound?

> MR. CHU

Ah, I don't really care.

> JIA-CHIEN

Ha! Another daughter!

INTERIOR. DINING/KITCHEN ROOM. EVENING.

He looks over the packed boxes.

> JIA-CHIEN
> *(from the kitchen)*

Have a seat. Dinner's almost ready.

Close on the delicious food prepared on the table.

He tastes the soup, frowning in thought. He tastes it again. She notices his reaction to it.

> JIA-CHIEN
> *(getting defensive)*

The soup—is there something the matter?

> MR. CHU

No, of course not. Delicious. And yet . . .

> JIA-CHIEN

Yes?

MR. CHU

Perhaps a bit too much ginger in the soup. If you use too much, its medicinal qualities are rendered useless.

JIA-CHIEN
(annoyed, tasting the soup herself)
I beg to differ—there is not too much ginger in the soup. This is the same recipe as mother always used to make, and I remember you bickering and moaning about it way back then. You are simply too timid in your use of ginger.

MR. CHU

I certainly have the right to—

JIA-CHIEN
—Don't try to boss me around the kitchen as you—

MR. CHU
(putting down his spoon)
—I'm not bossing anybody! I simply made a minor criticism about a slight taste of too much ginger, a taste that, a taste—

He stops mid sentence, almost in shock.

JIA-CHIEN
Yes? A taste?

>MR. CHU
>*(with quiet intensity)*

Jia-Chien, your soup!

He lifts the bowl up to his nose, and inhales deeply. He puts the bowl carefully down in front of him and slowly puts the spoon into it.

>JIA-CHIEN
>*(confused—not yet understanding, but—)*

What about the soup?

>MR. CHU
>*(still quietly)*

Your soup, Jia-Chien, I taste it. I can taste it.

>JIA-CHIEN
>*(very quietly—realizing the importance)*

You can taste?

An almost-tearful smile spreads on his face.

>MR. CHU

I can taste it.

He sips again from the soup.

They continue to eat. She watches him from the corner of her eye.

He takes a last spoonful from the bowl.

He holds up the near-empty bowl to her.

                                        MR. CHU
     Some more, please.

She stands and takes the bowl and ladles out some more soup for him.

As she hands him back the bowl, he takes the bowl in one hand and touches her hand with the other.

                                        MR. CHU
     Daughter.

She modestly lowers her eyes downwards.

                                        JIA-CHIEN
     Father.

We sit and observe them from afar in this pose for a few more seconds.

If we were close enough, we could see them crying.

The
Recipes

FOUR KINDS OF VEGETABLES

INGREDIENTS

   1 *can baby corn*
  14 *pieces Chinese green cabbage*
   2 *cups chicken stock*
   2 *tablespoons Chinese hot oil*
  12 *black mushrooms*
   1 *tablespoon soy sauce*
   8 *plum tomatoes*
   1 *tablespoon cornstarch*
    salt to taste

DIRECTIONS

- Simmer baby corn and cabbage in soup stock for two minutes. Season with salt. Drain, preserving the stock.
- Stir-fry black mushrooms in 2 tablespoons hot oil, season with 1 tablespoon soy sauce, cook for $^1/_2$ minute. Mix cornstarch with $^1/_2$ teaspoon water, add to the mushrooms, and cook for another $^1/_2$ minute.
- Simmer tomatoes in the soup stock for two minutes. Peel. Cut into halves.
- Group each vegetable on a plate, forming a circle. Serves five to six as an appetizer or side dish.

CHICKEN & CUCUMBER COLD SALAD

INGREDIENTS

2 chicken breasts, skin removed

2 cucumbers

6 tablespoons soy sauce

2 tablespoons vinegar

1 teaspoon sugar

2 tablespoons sesame oil

2 teaspoons minced garlic

2 scallions, chopped

¹/₂ cup carrots, shredded

DIRECTIONS

- Put chicken in boiling water, cook over medium heat for 15 minutes. Take out, let cool and shred (or tear by hand).
- Cut the cucumbers, skin and all, lengthwise into strips and put the strips in a large bowl.
- Put chicken shreds on cucumber, mix the soy sauce, vinegar, sugar, sesame oil and garlic to make the sauce, and pour on top. Sprinkle scallions and carrots on top and serve. Serves four as an appetizer.

MINCED SHRIMP IN LETTUCE

INGREDIENTS

1 pound prawns, or other shrimp
$1/2$ teaspoon salt
1 teaspoon cornstarch
2 Yiou-Tias, or "Chinese donuts"
    (long pieces of fried dough, found
    in Chinese specialty stores)
2 tablespoons peanut oil
$1/3$ cup chopped onions
$1/3$ cup chopped white leeks
$1/3$ cup peas (fresh or frozen)
head of iceberg lettuce
Chinese chili oil

SEASONING

4 green onions (scallions), chopped
1 teaspoon minced ginger
1 tablespoon soy sauce
1 tablespoon chicken stock (or water)
pinch of white pepper
$1/2$ teaspoon sesame oil

DIRECTIONS

- Clean and shell the shrimp, pat dry. Cut into small pieces and marinate for ten minutes in salt and cornstarch (mixed with $1/4$ teaspoon water).
- Cut Yiou-Tias into one-inch sections, fry in chili oil until crisp. Pat dry, flatten with a spatula or the side of a chopping knife, and tear or cut into small pieces.
- Fry shrimp in chili oil, stirring until they change color, about 1 minute.
- Fry onions in peanut oil in a separate pan for 2-3 minutes. Add shrimp, then seasoning; mix until coated. Mix with Yiou-Tias.
- Wash the lettuce and tear the leaves off, keeping them whole.
- Serve the shrimp wrapped in lettuce leaves. Serves four to six.

NOTE: If you can't find Yiou-Tias or wish to leave them out, the shrimp alone is still delicious!

STEAMED CHICKEN
WITH BLACK MUSHROOMS

INGREDIENTS

> 3 *chicken legs*
> 6 *dried black mushrooms*
> 2 *teaspoons soy sauce*
> $^1/_2$ *teaspoon rice wine*
> 1 *teaspoon cornstarch*
> 1 *teaspoon water*
> 2 *teaspoons minced green onions (scallions)*

DIRECTIONS

- Remove skin from chicken legs and cut them in half vertically, chopping straight through the bone.
- Soak mushrooms in water until soft, discard stems and cut the tops in half.
- In a large bowl mix chicken, mushrooms, cornstarch and seasonings together. Marinate for $^1/_2$ hour.
- Steam the ingredients over high heat for 20 minutes. Turn off heat, sprinkle with green onions. Serves three to four.

Stir Fried Taiwanese Clams

INGREDIENTS

2 pounds clams
2 small, fresh, sweet red peppers
8 leaves fresh basil
2 tablespoons soy sauce
2 tablespoons white wine
1 teaspoon minced garlic
1 teaspoon sesame oil
3 tablespoons peanut oil for cooking

DIRECTIONS

- Clean the clams by scrubbing them under cool running water with a vegetable brush.
- Cut red peppers into sections. Mix in a separate bowl with basil, soy sauce, wine, garlic and sesame oil.
- Heat the peanut oil in a wok or large frying pan. When the oil is hot add the clams and the sauce and mix. Cover and simmer over a low heat until the clams open. Serves four as an appetizer. Pour over rice or noodles to serve as a main course.

CHIN-HUA CHICKEN

INGREDIENTS

    2 green onions (scallions)
    3 nickel-sized slices fresh ginger
    1 chicken (3-4 pounds), cut into large pieces
  2¹/₂ cups chicken stock
    4 ounces Chinese ham, sliced ¹/₂ " wide
    ¹/₂ teaspoon salt
    2 teaspoons cornstarch paste
    ¹/₂ pound mustard or other greens (optional)

DIRECTIONS

- Bring ten cups of water to a boil, with green onions (whole) and ginger slices. Cook the chicken pieces in the water for 10 minutes, flipping the pieces if necessary. Turn the heat off and let the chicken sit, covered, for another ten minutes.
- Drain the chicken, cut the meat off the bone and into pieces 1" wide and 2" long.
- Boil 1¹/₂ cups chicken stock, remove from the flame and add the chicken and ham slices, letting them soak in the stock for 5 minutes. Discard the stock.
- Boil the remainder of the stock, season with the salt and thicken with cornstarch (mix cornstarch with 2 teaspoons of water before adding to the stock). Pour over the chicken.
- Boil the greens, and arrange them around the chicken and ham pieces on a platter. Serves 4-5.

THE
WEDDING
BANQUET

❁

The cast in alphabetical order

Dion Birney	ANDREW
Jeanne Kuo Chang	WAI TUNG'S SECRETARY
Winston Chao	WAI TUNG
Paul Chen	GUEST
May Chin	WEI WEI
Chung-Wei Chou	CHEF
Yun Chung	GUEST
Ho-Mean Fu	GUEST
Michael Gaston	JUSTICE OF THE PEACE
Ah-Leh Gua	MRS. GAO
Jeffrey Howard	STREET MUSICIAN
Theresa Hou	FEMALE CASHIER
Yung-Teh Hsu	BOB LAW
Jean Hu	GUEST
Albert Huang	GUEST
Neal Huff	STEVE
Anthony "Iggy" Ingoglia	RESTAURANT MGR.
Eddie Johns	HASKELL
Thomas Koo	GUEST
Chih Kuan	GRANNY TIEN
Robert Larenquent	HISPANIC MAN
Neal Lee	WAITER
Mason C. Lee	BABY
Dean Li	DIRECTOR WANG
Mitchell Lichtenstein	SIMON
Jennifer Lin	GUEST
Sihung Lung	MR. GAO
John Nathan	JOE
Francis Pan	GUEST
Neal Peng	GUEST
Tien Pien	OLD CHEN
Marny Pocato	MIRIAM
Tonia Rowe	SIMON'S NURSE
Chung-Hsien Su	STUDIO PHOTOGRAPHER
Patricial Sullivan	MARLANE
Elizabeth Yang	GUEST
Vanessa Yang	MAO
Wei-Huang Yang	GUEST
Pelde Yao	EGG HEAD

INTERIOR. GYM. DAY.

The screen is totally black. An old woman's clear and calm voice is heard.

MRS. GAO
(off screen)
It's been a long time since I last wrote you. My shoulder is acting up
again. I don't want to lift a pen. . . . So I recorded this cassette. This
way you can hear Ma's voice but don't have to deal with phone bills.

*Dissolve into the face of a young man on a stairmaster machine. Wai-Tung Gao
is a clean-cut, handsome thirty-year-old, wearing headphones tied to a
Walkman around his waist. We follow Wai-Tung while the head credits roll.*

MRS. GAO
(off screen)
Everyone says the pain is a sign of old age and that I will go away in a
couple of years. I hope so.

Wai-Tung, lifting a free weight, smirks at this.

MRS. GAO
(off screen)
Pa is acting very strange ever since he retired from the military. He was
a general commanding tens of thousands of soldiers. Now he only has
me and Old Chang to command at home. He's become very sensitive
and excitable.

Wai-Tung takes a breather, stretching on a mat.

MRS. GAO
(off screen)
Well, maybe it's because I am getting old. Your dad is getting even
older. Anyway, you're not getting any younger yourself. Why haven't
you got any plans for marriage? Your dad came to Taiwan from
Mainland China all by himself and you're his only precious son. Don't
be such a snob, O.K.?

*Wai-Tung is waiting for a machine, which is being used by a gorgeous blonde
woman. Wai-Tung gives her a cursory glance.*

MRS. GAO
(off screen)
We've enrolled you into Taipei's most exclusive singles club.

Wai-Tung climbs onto the machine and begins exercising.

> MRS. GAO
> *(off screen)*

They will send you a computer form to fill out. Tell them what's your ideal mate. All of the girls applying to the call-a-mate club have impeccable backgrounds. They are all well educated, and elegant—just like Mrs. Qian's daughter, the one you didn't want to marry. Promise me, my son. Stop being so choosy.

Close on Wai-Tung—his face is twisted with exertion.

Credits end.

INTERIOR. SIMON'S CLINIC. DAY.

Simon, white, handsome in a boyish, gentle way, is working at his job as a physical therapist. He attends to Miriam, a middle-aged woman, explaining the physical therapy exercises. He drops her leg in mock exasperation.

> SIMON

As a great Chinese poet once said *(He quotes Wang Wei in broken, heavily accented Chinese)*:
> "The green mountain stays young forever,
> Only snow makes its head turn white.
> Calm water has no worries,
> But the wind wrinkles its face."

> MIRIAM

What's that supposed to mean?

> SIMON

It means if you don't zen out you'll be murdered by your physical therapist.

A nurse enters the room.

> NURSE

Simon, there's a call for you.

INTERIOR. OFFICE. DAY. (CONTINUED)

Simon picks up the phone.

> SIMON

Hello? Hello?

EXTERIOR. N.Y.C. STREET PHONE BOOTH. DAY.

Intercut N.Y.C. phone booth on street, where Wai-Tung can barely hear because of a street musician playing an accordion in front of him.

                          WAI-TUNG
                    (to the street musician)
    Here, if I give you a buck, will you stop playing for a minute?

The guy takes the buck.

                          WAI-TUNG
    Simon?

                          SIMON
    Yeah, where are you?

                          WAI-TUNG
    In the city. Come in and meet me, I'll take you out to dinner.

                          SIMON
    Uh . . .

                          WAI-TUNG
    You still mad?

                          SIMON
    It's just we've been planning this trip for months—all you had to do was
    tell me that—

                          WAI-TUNG
    —But I can't control when zoning boards meet . . . We'll get the time
    together, I promise.

The nurse comes into the office, looking for some papers.

                          SIMON
    Look, just come home tonight. We'll talk about it later.

                          WAI-TUNG
    Sure. I'm going by the Williamsburg building first, be home by seven.

Wai-Tung hangs up the phone and taps the shoulder of the street musician who's been standing by. The musician launches into his song again, as Wai-Tung walks off.

EXTERIOR. BROOKLYN BRIDGE. DAY.

Wai-Tung, crossing the bridge on foot, bumps into another Chinese man, Law (who we will see later at the wedding).

LAW

Hey, it's you— . . . Wai-Tung! Damn, what a coincidence. You live in Brooklyn now?

Wai-Tung looks annoyed and a bit nervous.

WAI-TUNG

No—I live in Manhattan.

LAW

What are you up to now? How long has it been? I think the last time I saw you was after I had the operation, right? *(holds up his hand)* See, they put thirty-three different pieces of wire in there *(Wai-Tung looks disgusted as Law jiggles his hand)* but it's hardly noticeable, although *(pulling down his collar)* you can see where they grafted the skin—

WAI-TUNG

I'm sorry, I'm late as it is. Call me at the office.

Wai-Tung shakes his hand and walks on.

LAW

Let's get together some time!

INTERIOR. HOUSE. EVENING.

Simon scoops out another piece of pizza for Wai-Tung. There are candles and half-empty wine glasses.

Simon watches Wai-Tung eat.

SIMON

You're eating too fast.

WAI-TUNG

I'm nervous. If they let me convert the Hudson building, I'll make millions. If not, we couldn't even afford a vacation in the Poconos.

SIMON

What's the point of being able to afford a vacation when you won't take the time off to have one?

WAI-TUNG
(still eating)

Hmm.

SIMON

Speaking of which, Steve and Andrew just got back from Belize.

WAI TUNG

Hmm.

SIMON

They hated the hotel.

WAI-TUNG

Was that the one we were going to stay in?

SIMON

Yeah. So I guess it's great we didn't go.

Wai-Tung stops eating, looks up at Simon, puts his hand in his.

WAI-TUNG

Look, Simon, I'm really sorry. But I've made up my mind.

Simon looks nervous, awaiting some sort of pronouncement.

WAI-TUNG

I'm taking you to Paris. In September, right after the zoning hearing. It will be a birthday present.

SIMON
(playfully throwing his napkin at Wai-Tung)
You're such a jerk.

EXTERIOR. IN FRONT OF HOUSE. MORNING.

A weekend. Simon is taking out the garbage when Steve, early thirties, handsome, rides up on his bicycle, a tennis racquet strapped across his back.

STEVE

Hey you homo! *(Simon looks up, startled)* What are you doing in this neighborhood? Hello.

SIMON
(laughing)
Don't joke about it. You know the Winchells down the street there? Check them out.

He gestures down and across the street, where a prototypical American middle-aged John Birch-type couple are standing tinkering on their steps. An American flag hangs from their house. The couple is pretending not to look at Simon and Steve.

STEVE

Cute. So do you and the mighty Wai want to go shoot some hoops later, like, I don't know, maybe around 2?

SIMON

Oh, uh, Wai has to run stuff over to Williamsburg and deal with some tenant stuff. I might be able to make it though. I'll call you.

STEVE
(riding off)

Just show up! See ya!

SIMON

See ya.

Down the street, as Steve rides by the couple, he gives them a little wave.

EXTERIOR. WILLIAMSBURG BUILDING. DAY.

Wai-Tung is angrily moving trash cans back against the building. A young white guy, rather scruffy-looking, is standing next to him, watching and kind of helping, but not really.

WAI-TUNG
(brushing off his hands)
If they're not off the sidewalk by 10:30, I get a ticket.

JOE

I'm sorry boss.

WAI-TUNG

You're sorry! Those tickets cost me $175 bucks. I get another one, it's coming out of your salary!

Wai-Tung walks to the door and buzzes.

WEI-WEI
(voice off)

Who is it?

WAI-TUNG

It's the evil landowner.

INTERIOR. APARTMENT/ART STUDIO. DAY. (INTERCUT)

WEI-WEI
The sixth floor has been liberated!

INTERCUT WAI-TUNG STANDING AT THE DOORWAY, STILL WAITING.

WEI-WEI
(voice off)
O.K., since you're so handsome, you can come in.

The door finally buzzes.

INTERIOR. APARTMENT STAIRWAY. DAY. (CONTINUED)

Wai-Tung walks up the stairway.

INTERIOR. APARTMENT/ART STUDIO. DAY. (CONTINUED)

*Wai-Tung is looking at a canvas, holding it at arm's length. There's loud
Taiwanese music playing, over which they speak.*

WAI-TUNG
This is not rent.

WEI-WEI
Simon says that in ten years, my paintings will be worth tens of
thousands of dollars.

WAI-TUNG
Simon is not your landlord. I am. And I don't understand modern art.

WEI-WEI
But you like me.

Wai-Tung just looks around at the mess.

> WAI-TUNG

What a dump.

> WEI-WEI

It's my fate, I always fall in love with handsome gay men.

> WAI-TUNG

You haven't the slightest interest in me. Don't try to dump your paintings on me for rent.

> WAI-TUNG
> *(spotting the stereo)*

What's this noise?

Wei-Tung turns it off, and now all the noise from the rest of the building and neighborhood can be heard.

> WEI-WEI

Sorry, it's to block the noise from outside. I can't concentrate.

> WAI-TUNG

You like Taiwanese pop music?

> WEI-WEI

Anything to block the noise.

Wai-Tung looks at the painting she's working on.

> WAI-TUNG

What's this painting called?

> WEI-WEI

"Heat." If you shut this heat off, the whole building will be without hot water.

> WAI-TUNG

Then don't touch it.

> WEI-WEI

Wai-Tung, can't you spend a little money to fix it—it's so hot in here. It's inhumane. How can anyone live in conditions like this?

Wai-Tung, starting to sweat, walks to the window.

> WAI-TUNG

It's not a residential building. That's why the rent is so cheap.

He tries to open the window, without success.

WEI-WEI

I've tried it for a year—it can't be opened.

Wai-Tung has nothing to say. He walks to the stove and sees a melting bar of chocolate in a pan of day-old cooked rice.

WAI-TUNG
(grossed out by the food smell)

What is this?

WEI-WEI
(in English)

My depression special.

WAI-TUNG

Are you that poor?

WEI-WEI

No, I'm just depressed. The immigration people came yesterday. Lucky I was late to work.

WAI-TUNG

As usual.

WEI-WEI

But they took Emily away. If they get me the next time I'll be able to meet Emily in Shanghai. *(pausing)* Emily was my best friend. Now I am out of work and out of friends.

Wei-Wei begins to cry quietly.

WAI-TUNG

I'm sorry.

He puts his hand on her shoulder. She rests her head on his neck, still gently crying, holding him just a little to tightly. When her embrace starts too feel more romantic than sisterly, Wai-Tung pushes back.

WAI-TUNG

You have no relatives here?

WEI-WEI

They were nice enough to sponsor me here—I can't trouble them again. I'm not like you, a rich American citizen.

WAI-TUNG

I don't have as much money as you think. All my money is stuck in stinking real estate like this!

Wai-Tung, embarrassed, fidgets around the room, tripping over tequila bottles and other garbage, then picks up the painting.

WEI-WEI
Your only investment in this building is in my loft.

WAI-TUNG
(admiring the painting, a bit falsely, trying to cheer her up)
I think I kind of like this one. It's pretty good. I'll take it as rent. It should cover the last two months' rent as well.

WEI-WEI
(sweetly)
Thank you, Wai-Tung. And Wai-Tung, when do you think you'll be fixing that bathroom sink?

Wai-Tung is about to say something, thinks better of it, and heads down the hallway.

WEI-WEI
(after him)
Say hi to Simon! He's a lucky to have a handsome and wealthy boyfriend! Ask him to find one for me too! Then I can pay your rent!

INTERIOR. HOUSE. EVENING.

Wai-Tung is sitting at his desk, filling out a form, when Simon comes up to see what he's doing.

WAI-TUNG

My perfect woman.

SIMON

What? Another one? Don't those things cost a fortune?

WAI-TUNG

Yes, but how can I tell them to stop paying for them?

SIMON

Why don't you just tell them? Shit.

Wai-Tung pays no attention.

SIMON

No, really, Wai. Look at yourself—your parents send you a form in the mail and you practically pee in your pants. You know, you are an adult—as a matter of fact, you're practically middle aged.

WAI-TUNG
(half laughing)

Fuck you!

SIMON
(reading the form)

Alright, let me check this out—education, right?

WAI-TUNG

Yes.

Simon sits next to him.

SIMON

Well, she must have a Ph.D.

WAI-TUNG

No, two Ph.D.'s.

He writes it down.

SIMON

One in Physics.

WAI-TUNG
(laughing)

And she should be an opera singer!

SIMON

And six feet tall!

>   WAI-TUNG
> Let's not go overboard—she's Chinese, after all. Five foot nine. And she
> should speak five languages.

They look up, laughing, at each other. Then Wai-Tung changes to a more serious expression.

>   WAI-TUNG
> You're right, it's kind of stupid, all these lies. But I'm used to it.

>   SIMON
> Hey. I got you a little present.

>   WAI-TUNG
> Me? Why?

Simon has gotten up and returned with a small wrapped gift.

>   SIMON
> Shut up and open it.

Wai-Tung opens it up. It's a small cellular phone. He's delighted.

>   SIMON
> For the busy entrepreneur. Go ahead, try it.

Wai-Tung dials a number. The house phone rings, and Simon answers it.

>   SIMON
> Hello?

>   WAI-TUNG
> Thanks.

>   SIMON
> You're welcome.

>   WAI-TUNG
> I love you.

>   SIMON
> I love you too.

They kiss.

INTERIOR. WAI-TUNG'S OFFICE. DAY.

Wai-Tung sits in a small cluttered office, as his secretary, a middle-aged Chinese woman, files papers. He is talking on the phone while opening mail.

WAI-TUNG

Yes, but if I sell it to the S corporation, and they re-appraise the building, it'll kill me at tax time.

He holds his hand over the receiver, while waving a letter he has just opened at his secretary, who takes it.

WAI-TUNG
(to secretary)

Fax that to Chow. *(back into the phone)* Okay, I'll sign it if you say so, but if it costs me, it's coming out of your salary!

The secretary, in an almost scared tone of voice, addresses Wai-Tung.

SECRETARY

Boss, Miss Wei-Wei Gu called when you went to the toilet. She's complaining that the heat is on.

WAI-TUNG

The heat, what heat? It's June!

As he speaks he opens a small package from his mother—another tape. He tosses it on top of a big "in" pile of documents and phone messages.

INTERIOR. GYM. DAY.

Wai-Tung works out, listening to another tape from his mother.

MRS. GAO
(off screen)
Son, you must be surprised to get another cassette from me so soon. I have good news. Call-a-mate club is really something. They've already found a near perfect match for you. She's tall. But she only has one doctorate degree. Because she sings opera, she speaks five languages! Your dad and I have decided to give you a big gift. We've arranged for her to go to New York for a visit. Her name is Wu Ren. But everyone calls her by her nickname, Little Sister Mao. She should be in New York in about two weeks. She'll be staying with her cousin I want you to pick her up at the airport. Aren't you excited? I know we are.

Wai-Tung practically falls off his stairmaster.

WAI-TUNG
Shit!

EXTERIOR. AIRPORT PARKING LOT. DAY.

Wai-Tung, struggling with several bags and suitcases, is walking haltingly, a young woman following behind him, carrying just her purse.

MAO
Oh, I'm exhausted. I'm so sorry to trouble you like this, brother Gao.

WAI-TUNG
Sister Mao, how's Mister Mao and . . . I mean how are your parents?

MAO
They are fine, thank you.

WAI-TUNG
(catching his breath)
Did you remember to bring your cousin's address with you.

MAO
Of course! I'm not a kid, you know.

WAI-TUNG
No you're not. Sister Mao, your luggage is so heavy. Why didn't you use cargo service to send some of the stuff directly to your cousin's place?

MAO
I did! Half the stuff here is for you from your mother.

WAI-TUNG
Oh, I'm sorry. In that case, I'll treat you to a nice dinner tonight. This luggage is really heavy.

MAO
(smiling)

No, it's not. Where is the car?

WAI-TUNG

Here. . . .

EXTERIOR. HIP RESTAURANT. EVENING.

Wai-Tung and Mao are seated at a trendy restaurant, located on a dock overlooking Manhattan. They're both bored and preoccupied.

WAI-TUNG

This is your first time in America?

MAO

No. I sang at the San Francisco Opera for two years..

WAI-TUNG

Ah, yes, yes. Opera, yes.

MAO

And you are an opera fan?

WAI-TUNG
(lying)

Yes.

A lull.

MAO

Huh.

WAI-TUNG

Yes?

MAO

Nothing.

Wai-Tung looks anxiously around.

WAI-TUNG

The service here is terrible. *(pause)* So, you've met my parents.

MAO

Just your mom. Your dad was still in the hospital.

> WAI-TUNG
> *(shocked)*
The hospital? When was he in the hospital?

> MAO
About two weeks ago. He had a stroke. You didn't know?

> WAI-TUNG
No.

> MAO
I'm sorry. Me and my big mouth. Mrs. Gao probably didn't want you to worry.

> WAI-TUNG
No . . . thanks for letting me know.

> MAO
Mrs. Gao also told me that there was this huge traffic jam when Mr. Gao was still in the ambulance. They couldn't get to the hospital. Mr. Gao was in a lot of pain. He was half numb. He was really suffering and looked as though he was going to give up. But he hung on for his one last wish and finally made it to the hospital.

> WAI-TUNG
What last wish?

> MAO
To hold his grandchild.

Wai-Tung stares out over the water and doesn't say a word. Mao feels even more uncomfortable.

> MAO
He's going to be fine, don't worry.

She lightly touches his hand to reassure him.

The waitress arrives, witnessing the apparently romantic scene.

> WAITRESS
May I take your order?

Wai-Tung looks up to discover that the waitress is none other than . . .

> WAI-TUNG
Wei-Wei!

WEI-WEI

Wai-Tung!

WAI-TUNG
(trying to crack a joke)
Wei-Wei, you got a new job?

WEI-WEI

So what if I did?

She gives Sister Mao a dirty look.

WAI-TUNG
(nervous)
This is Miss Wu from Taipei. She's an opera singer. Wei-Wei is
squatting—er, is renting an apartment of mine—uh, that I own.

Wei-Wei is obviously misreading the situation.

WEI-WEI
I spoke to Simon on the phone today.

WAI-TUNG
(desperately trying to hide his gay identity)
Simon? Oh, Simon! How is he?

WEI-WEI
How is he? He really likes the painting I gave you. He said you had some
family business to take care of today. So this is the family business?
Does Simon know what you're up to?

Mao looks amused.

WAI-TUNG
This . . . is not what you think.

WEI-WEI
(yelling)
Telling me you were gay and I always believed you! Why didn't you just
come right out and tell me you don't like me?

The restaurant manager arrives.

MANAGER
Is there some kind of problem here?

Tears leap into Wei-Wei's eyes.

WEI-WEI

Poor Simon—I pity him.

In frustration she throws her towel and pad down and runs from the restaurant.

The manager chases after her.

MANAGER

Hey, wait—shit, why can't they quit after dinner?

Mao just smiles at Wai-Tung, who doesn't know whether to chase after Wei-Wei or stay. Finally he slinks back down into his seat.

EXTERIOR. SOCRATES SCULPTURE PARK. EVENING.

Wai-Tung and Mao walk along a pathway, talking in a relaxed, friendly way.

WAI-TUNG

So why did you join the call-a-mate club?

MAO

I'm not so ridiculous. My mom did it for me. Just like you, I have a white boyfriend. And I don't have the guts to tell my parents either.

They pause by the water.

WAI-TUNG

Where did you learn how to sing?

MAO

Dong-Wu University, music department.

WAI-TUNG

You don't talk like an opera singer.

MAO

A talking voice does not necessary sound like a singing voice.

WAI-TUNG

Is that right?

MAO

Are you really an opera fan?

WAI-TUNG

No.

MAO

Thought so. Pity.

Mao raises her arms dramatically and begins to sing an aria from Madame Butterfly as Wai-Tung stands by, embarrassed.

INTERIOR. STAIRWELL/HALLWAY. NIGHT.

Simon and Wai-Tung are hauling up an air-conditioner.

INTERIOR. WEI-WEI'S APARTMENT. NIGHT.

Simon and Wai-Tung push the air-conditioner into Wei-Wei's apartment, sweating and out of breath.

> WEI-WEI
>
> You must forgive me. I'm so ashamed. When Simon told me the story, I felt like jumping off the Brooklyn Bridge.

> WAI-TUNG
>
> No, it's for me to apologize—you've been having so many troubles, and all I do is pressure you for rent. Here, I've brought you an air-conditioner.

> WEI-WEI
> *(suspicious, checking it out)*
> But the electricity costs . . .

Wai-Tung heads for the bathroom.

> SIMON
>
> Anyway, Wai and I would like to invite you out to dinner.

> WEI-WEI
>
> Ah, it will be my farewell dinner.

> SIMON
>
> Your what?

> WEI-WEI
>
> Really, I can't last any longer. No money, no job, and no green card—no stupid American will marry me.

> SIMON
>
> Well, what about Boris, I thought he was going to marry you.

> WEI-WEI
>
> He was—but he wanted $5,000 dollars!

> SIMON
>
> What? What about Andre? That guy you were seeing?

WEI-WEI

He wanted to marry me too, but it turns out he's Albanian and doesn't have a green card himself. *(pause)* I'm such an idiot!

Simon gives her a look.

INTERIOR. BEDROOM. NIGHT.

Wai-Tung lays in bed as Simon jabs at him.

WAI-TUNG

I said forget about it.

SIMON

But don't you see, this way Wei-Wei can stay in the states and paint, and you can finally get your parents off your back.

WAI-TUNG

Forget about it.

SIMON

Look, we can move her into the basement room until after the immigration exam. Take some photos, send them back to your mom and dad—and perfect.

WAI-TUNG

Forget it.

SIMON

Hey, and as a married couple, you'll be able to take a big tax break.

Wai-Tung perks up. Simon smiles.

Montage.

Steve and Andrew help Wei-Wei and Simon move stuff out of the car.

Wai-Tung looks on in slight disdain as Wei-Wei's paintings are carted off to the back room.

INTERIOR. MASTER BEDROOM. DAY.

Simon is giving Wei-Wei a tour of the house. They stand next to a chest of drawers.

SIMON

Wai-Tung's clothes. Shirts here, underwear—he wears jockey but he sleeps in boxer shorts—and here's all the stuff he gets from his parents—mega polyester, but he saves the shit religiously.

INTERIOR. LIVING ROOM. DAY.

> SIMON

The couch is his own little world. Here, piles of unread magazines—World Trade, Advocate, GQ, Fortune—he's such a disgusting yuppie, and, of course, the phone, which he hogs like a total pig, extra pillows, 'cause he likes to drop off to sleep here. Sometimes I have to practically carry him up to bed.

INTERIOR. KITCHEN. DAY.

> SIMON

He showers in the morning except when he goes right to the gym, which is usually when he's in a bad mood or we've been fighting. He doesn't smoke or drink—unless we've been fighting or he's in a bad mood. *(opening fridge)* And no junk food either—

> WEI-WEI
> *(writing it all down)*

—Unless you've been fighting or he's in a bad mood.

INTERIOR. BACK ROOM. DAY.

Wei-Wei lies comfortably on the couch. A soft wind blows through her hair.

INTERIOR. KITCHEN. MORNING.

Simon and Wei-Wei sit at the breakfast table, going over her notes for the immigration exam.

> WEI-WEI

On his right side?

> SIMON

Uh huh, the birthmark is on his right side. The mole is on his left side.

Simon pats his behind to show her where.

> WEI-WEI

Do the questions really get this personal?

> SIMON

Yes they do—and if you don't pass—

> WEI-WEI

Oh I'll pass!

Just then, Wai-Tung enters the kitchen, rushing to get a cup of coffee before leaving for work.

WEI-WEI
Let's see. Today is Friday. You are wearing blue jockey shorts.

Wai-Tung slams his coffee down on the counter.

INTERIOR. BEDROOM. NIGHT.

A loud phone ring wakes Simon and Wai-Tung. Wai-Tung turns on the lamp. The alarm clock reads three-thirty.

SIMON
Jesus Christ!

WAI-TUNG
(picking up phone)
Hello—

OPERATOR
(voice off)
Long distance from Taiwan. Is Mr. Gao there?

WAI-TUNG
This is he.

OPERATOR
(voice off)
Go ahead.

MRS. GAO
(voice off)
Hello, Wai-Tung?

WAI-TUNG
Oh ma, it's you.

MRS. GAO
(voice off)
Hold on . . .

WAI-TUNG
Hello?

MR. GAO
(voice off)
Wai-Tung?

WAI-TUNG

Pa? How are you doing?

MR. GAO
(voice off)

We are overjoyed, son!

WAI-TUNG

So you got my letter?

MR. GAO
(voice off)

But why did you keep the news from us for so long?

We follow Simon as he gets up to go to the bathroom, so that we can hear only Wai-Tung's side of the conversation.

WAI-TUNG

Like I told you in the letter, Wei-Wei is from Mainland. We've been dating for two years and decided to settle down just recently. I didn't want to tell you before because I was afraid you wouldn't approve.

A pause.

WAI-TUNG

What?! You are coming here? The fifteenth? No, . . . of course I want you to be in charge of the wedding. I know it's once in a lifetime.

Simon flushes, walks back into the bedroom and sits at the edge of the bed, watching Wai-Tung.

WAI-TUNG

But I told you why in the letter. Pa is still recovering and he has hypertension. You shouldn't be making such a long trip.

Simon crawls back into bed, trying to understand the Chinese conversation with one ear. He takes a guide book of Paris from his night table and pretends to read it.

WAI-TUNG

What if . . . stop talking like that. Of course you'll live to see your grandchild . . . I won't disappoint you . . . I'm just saying why be so formal. Ma? Ma, go talk to dad. Tell him not to be so sensitive. All right, all right. I'll talk to you tomorrow. OK, OK. I'll call you tomorrow. Bye.

He hangs up and turns to Simon.

WAI-TUNG
Did you understand any of that?

SIMON
Unfortunately, I think so.

WAI-TUNG
(flopping himself back down into the bed)
This was your big idea.

SIMON
How long are they coming for?

WAI-TUNG
Just a short visit—two weeks!

Montage/House.

Out goes the gay stuff, and up goes the Chinese calligraphy, as Simon, Wai-Tung, and Wei-Wei prepare for the parents' arrival.

EXTERIOR. AIRPORT. DAY.

A Boeing lands at JFK airport.

INTERIOR. AIRPORT. DAY.

Wai-Tung and Wei-Wei search among the crowd of passengers coming out of the customs gate.

WEI-WEI
God, this is nerve wracking.

WAI-TUNG
Relax, you know the saying, ''The bride must meet the in laws, no matter how ugly.''

WEI-WEI
And how about the ugly ''son-in-law''?

WAI-TUNG
Here they come!

Mr. and Mrs. Gao appear amid a crowd of people. They spot Wai-Tung immediately and wave. Wai-Tung smiles and goes up to meet them.

MRS. GAO
Oh Wai-Tung, we missed you so much.

WAI-TUNG
Are you tired?

MR. GAO
I slept through the whole trip. No jet lag.

MRS. GAO
I had no such luck. But I started feeling better the moment I saw you.

WAI-TUNG
You two lost a lot of weight! Looking good.

MRS. GAO
We're old.

MR. GAO
Wei-Wei didn't come?

WAI-TUNG
She's over there.

They search the crowd for her—spot her—and look her over from head to toe.

WEI-WEI
(coming up to meet them)
Mr. Gao, Mrs. Gao, nice to meet you.

Mr. and Mrs. Gao can't keep their eyes off Wei-Wei.

MR. GAO
. . . Hmm . . .

MRS. GAO
Prettier than in the pictures. You cut your hair?

MR. GAO
She looks better with short hair.

Wei-Wei lets her hair down for them.

MRS. GAO
Thank you for taking care of Wai-Tung.

WEI-WEI
No, he took care of me.

WAI-TUNG
Come on, let's not block traffic.

The Gaos head for the door while Wei-Wei grabs the luggage.

> WEI-WEI

Allow me.

EXTERIOR. AIRPORT PARKING LOT. DAY.

As the group walks to the car.

> MRS. GAO

Wai-Tung, where did you find such a beautiful wife?

> WAI-TUNG

I put an ad in the paper. I advertised an apartment for rent two years ago. Twelve people responded. I chose Wei-Wei.

> MR. GAO

Good. So my investment was worth it.

> MRS. GAO
> *(whispers to Mr. Gao)*

What do you think?

> MR. GAO
> *(watching her pull the luggage)*

She will have lots of babies.

Mrs. Gao hushes him.

INTERIOR. CAR. DAY.

Wai-Tung drives.

> MRS. GAO

Wei-Wei, how long have you been in America?

> WEI-WEI

Over three years. I never went back home.

> MRS. GAO

Who else is in your family?

> WEI-WEI

Pa, ma and a kid brother in high school.

> MR. GAO

What do your parents do?

> WAI-TUNG

Pa works in the hospital and Ma teaches high school art.

MR. GAO

That's good. According to tradition, we're supposed to bring the "gift of four colors" to your home and formally propose to your parents.

WEI-WEI

My parents are very easy going. They've seen Wai-Tung's pictures and heard me talk about him all the time. They both like Wai-Tung very much, it's just too inconvenient for them to come here from Mainland.

MR. GAO

That's too bad.

EXTERIOR. WAI-TUNG'S HOME. AFTERNOON.

The car pulls up in front of the house. Wei-Wei gets out and runs to the trunk to get the luggage.

INTERIOR. HOUSE. AFTERNOON.

Simon, hearing them arrive, comes out of the kitchen. Just before he reaches the door, he remembers to take his earring out and put it in his pocket.

The family enters.

WAI-TUNG

Pa, Ma, this is Simon, my roommate and landlord.

They all shake hands.

SIMON
(in very bad Chinese)
Welcome to home Mr. Gao, Mrs. Gao, it's pleasure to meet you.

MRS. GAO

You speak Chinese?

MR. GAO

Thank you for taking care of Wai-Tung and letting us stay here.

Simon stares blankly.

WAI-TUNG

Pa, he doesn't really understand.

MR. GAO

No?

WAI-TUNG

Just a little bit.

MRS. GAO

Then, tell him his house is beautiful!

SIMON

So, should I help with the stuff?

WAI-TUNG

Yeah, that'd be great.

MRS. GAO

Wai-Tung, how come you rent Simon's home and don't live in one of your own buildings?

WAI-TUNG

Ma, the buildings I bought are all dumps. You can't live in them. But Wei-Wei and I are looking for our own home. We'll move after we get married.

Everyone goes upstairs except Mr. Gao. He wanders through the living room, studying the furnishings, and then walks out onto the back porch.

EXTERIOR. BACKYARD. AFTERNOON.

Mr. Gao stands contemplating the Spring foliage. Wai-Tung comes back out to him.

WAI-TUNG

Pa.

MR. GAO

This place is nice.

WAI-TUNG

Yes, and the air is fresh.

MR. GAO

Wai-Tung, you're getting married. I have to tell you something. Do you know why I joined the military?

WAI-TUNG

You responded to General Chiang's call to join the army during the Sino-Japanese War.

MR. GAO

No. I wanted to run away from home. So I joined the army. Your grandpa had arranged a marriage for me. I got mad and just took off.

After the war, we fought the Communists. A relative escaped to Taiwan and brought me a letter from your grandpa. He told me that there was no longer a Gao family and that I should start my own family outside the mainland, to continue the family name. Son, imagine how I feel to be able to attend your wedding.

> WAI-TUNG

Pa, you really should have stayed home and rested.

Mr. Gao smiles, and, raising his fist, punches Wai-Tung's puffed out chest, in a gesture they've often repeated since Wai-Tung's childhood. Then he turns and walks back into the house with a hand on Wai-Tung's shoulder.

INTERIOR. KITCHEN. NIGHT.

A crackling and sizzling sound is heard as a big bunch of fresh bean sprouts is poured into a wok with red hot oil. Simon is pan-frying the bean sprouts as Wei-Wei watches. Mrs. Gao, just finished bathing, is coming downstairs to the kitchen. Simon and Wei-Wei, hearing her footsteps, switch places quickly and smoothly.

> SIMON
> *(whispering to Wei-Wei)*

Stir a little bit longer and then drain the juice.

Mrs. Gao walks up to the two of them.

> MRS. GAO

Thank you for cooking.

> WEI-WEI

Oh, it's nothing. Feel better after the hot bath?

> MRS. GAO

Yes!

> WEI-WEI

Where is pa? Dinner is almost ready.

> MRS. GAO

He's almost finished. Let me help with the settings.

> WEI-WEI

They're over here.

> MRS. GAO

Wai-Tung is lucky. He found a girl who still can cook.

Simon motions to Wei-Wei to pour out the juice. Wei-Wei clumsily tries to do so and almost pours everything out. Fortunately, Simon saves her by quickly using another spatula to block the bean sprouts from falling out.

INTERIOR. LIVING ROOM. NIGHT.

Wai-Tung and Mr. Gao come down to the living room together. Mr. Gao notices a framed piece of calligraphy hanging on the wall.

MR. GAO

When did I write this?

WAI-TUNG

You mailed it to me in March two years ago. I like this one the most. That's why I put it in the living room.

MR. GAO

This is a very good one. There is not one "loser" stroke. That's not easy to do.

Wei-Wei and Simon come into the living room from the kitchen.

WEI-WEI

Pa, dinner is ready.

SIMON

Dinner is ready. Let's eat.

WAI-TUNG

Pa, let's see how you like our cooking compared to Old Chang's.

WEI-WEI

Pa, of all the pieces of scrolls you've sent to Wai-Tung, this one I like best. It's really great art.

MR. GAO

How so?

WEI-WEI

The Wang Hsi Zhi school of calligraphy emphasizes harmony and nature—it's subtle yet substantive. Your Wang style of calligraphy reflects a beauty that comes from an impeccable structure combined with unrefined purity. Your writing flows naturally with Bei Qu Yi's poem. That's not a level of art often attained. Plus there isn't one "loser" stroke throughout. That demonstrates to me your steadiness. It's a sign of longevity.

Mr. Gao has on his face a smile stretching from ear to ear.

MR. GAO

Wai-Tung, she is more of an expert than you.

WAI-TUNG

What do you expect? She studies art.

Mrs. Gao comes out from the kitchen.

MRS. GAO

The food is getting cold. Let's eat.

MR. GAO

Wei-Wei, we give you so much more work to do.

WEI-WEI

Not at all, it's something I should do.

Mr. Gao heads toward the dining room in happy steps. The others follow. As they pass the sofa.

WEI-WEI
(to Mrs. Gao)

This is Wai-Tung's own little world. He sits here every day to read, make phone calls, listen to music. Sometimes he even sleeps here overnight.

INTERIOR. DINING ROOM. NIGHT

Mr. Gao is tasting a dish, as everyone watches expectantly, Simon in particular.

MR. GAO

Um . . . very good. Just the right amount of soda. The soaking time is perfect, too, which gives it just the right tenderness.

SIMON
(in English, to Wai-Tung)

He likes it?

WAI-TUNG

Yeah.

Simon is proud.

MR. GAO

Wei-Wei, you must have gone through a lot of trouble.

WEI-WEI

Not really. Anyway, it's not as good as old Chang's.

MR. GAO

Yours is better. He uses too much salt.

MRS. GAO

Old Chang has been our cook for over thirty years. He's from Sichuan.

SIMON

(to Wai-Tung, not understanding the Chinese)

What's she saying?

INTERIOR. KITCHEN. NIGHT.

Wai-Tung and Simon are washing dishes.

INTERIOR. MASTER BEDROOM. NIGHT.

Wei-Wei follows Mrs. Gao into the master bedroom. Mr. Gao follows them. Two large pieces of luggage are spread open on the bed. Mrs. Gao takes out a few treasures. She gives Wei-Wei first a small red envelope containing cash.

WEI-WEI

What is this?

MRS. GAO

This is our gift of the First Acquaintance to our daughter-in-law. Thank you for your taking care of Wai-Tung.

MR. GAO

We are handing him over to you. Wei-Wei, Wai-Tung is in your hands now.

WEI-WEI

Then I can't refuse it, can I?

MRS. GAO

This pearl necklace we bought in Japan during our vacation there last year. You can wear it at the wedding.

WEI-WEI

It's beautiful! Must be very expensive.

MRS. GAO

This is natural pearl, not the cultured ones.

Wei-Wei places it against her breast.

MRS. GAO

This we bought in Malaysia, red coral pin.

Wei-Wei is now painfully aware not only of the beautiful gifts, but of her own fraud in accepting them. She tries to hide her sadness.

WEI-WEI

Oh, this is gorgeous! This is too much.

MRS. GAO

We chose this top quality pure silk from Taiwan's biggest textile firm. Hey, do they make Chi Pao gowns in New York?

WEI-WEI

I think they do in Chinatown.

MRS. GAO

This is a Chi Pao bracelet that we bought from the best wholesale jeweler in Taipei. Go try this on. Can we find a place for alterations?

WEI-WEI

Probably in Chinatown.

MRS. GAO

This is really a piece of treasure. I brought this with me from the Mainland to Taiwan when I was young. Look at the quality of the material and workmanship. You can't find it anymore.

WEI-WEI

I'll go try it on.

MRS. GAO

Wait, one more. This gold bracelet is from Old Chang.

MR. GAO

Old Chang worked for us for over forty years. He raised Wai-Tung with us.

WEI-WEI

I don't know what to say . . . I'll go try on the Chi Pao.

MRS. GAO
(to her husband)
I told you she'd like it. And you said I shouldn't give away old clothes.

Wai-Tung and Simon come into the bedroom.

WAI-TUNG

Ma and pa, Simon has some gifts for you.

Simon gives them each a nicely wrapped box.

MR. GAO

You shouldn't have.

MRS. GAO

We are already staying in your home. How can we take gifts from you?

Simon speaks in broken Chinese.

SIMON

It's just a little something.

Mr. and Mrs. Gao open the boxes. For Mr. Gao there's an instrument for measuring blood pressure, and for Mrs. Gao a cosmetic cream.

SIMON

You . . . heart problem and you . . . blood pressure is
high . . . monitor your blood . . .

Mr. Gao is obviously not pleased.

SIMON

Mrs. Gao, this is protein facial cream . . . especially for older woman.
Massage face night before bed . . . helps prevent wrinkles.

Mrs. Gao has barely a smile.

MRS. GAO

You want me to be young forever.

SIMON

Yes, never get old, older . . . old . . . older.

Wai-Tung gives him a nudge.

Wei-Wei glides out of the bathroom wearing Mrs. Gao's Chi Pao.

WEI-WEI

Wai-Tung, look what ma gave me. The Chi Pao she wore when she was
young.

MR. GAO

Ha, ha, ha, ha . . .

WAI-TUNG

Look, it fits perfectly.

MRS. GAO

I just knew it would fit her. This is something a mother-in-law would
just know. It's a spiritual bond that passes on from generation to

generation. Wei-Wei, we are brought here by fate. You and Wai-Tung together. This is called, "fate will find you no matter how far apart". This is called "a world away is only a foot in distance."

The family gathers around the embarrassed Wei-Wei, as Simon, forgotten, looks on.

EXTERIOR. PROMENADE. DAY.

Wai-Tung jogs with his father along the river, amid the morning haze.

INTERIOR. KITCHEN. DAY.

Wei-Wei is frying eggs in the kitchen. Mrs. Gao is slicing oranges. Wei-Wei puts the broken pieces of fried egg onto a plate. She then opens the fridge to take out a grapefruit and a spoon from a drawer.

> WEI-WEI
> Ma, this is Wai-Tung's personal spoon.

Wai-Tung and Mr. Gao enter the kitchen.

> MR. GAO
> I feel great. We walked a full hour.

Mrs. Gao hands him a glass of juice and a pill. Mr. Gao places the pill in his mouth and drinks down the juice.

> MR. GAO
> I'll go wash up.

Mr. Gao leaves the kitchen and goes upstairs.

> WEI-WEI
> Wai-Tung, go wake up Simon.

Wai-Tung takes a look at the pathetically-fried eggs and makes a face at Wei-Wei.

> WEI-WEI
> What are you looking at? Never seen eggs over easy before?

Wai-Tung walks out of the kitchen laughing.

INTERIOR. SIMON'S DEN. DAY.

Simon is still in bed. Wai-Tung comes in, sits on the bed, and gives him a shoulder rub.

> WAI-TUNG
> Hey love muffin. Time to make a doughnut.

Simon opens his eyes with satisfaction then turns over.

> SIMON
> How was my performance on the first day?

> WAI-TUNG
> About a B plus. I don't know, we should have moved you out.

> SIMON
> We'll survive.

> WAI-TUNG
> Not if Wei-Wei keeps cooking.

INTERIOR. MASTER BEDROOM. DAY.

Wai-Tung leaves Simon's room and goes into the master bedroom.

> WAI-TUNG
> Pa . . .

Wai-Tung sees Mr. Gao slumped on a sofa. Eyes shut. Motionless. Wai-Tung walks up to him, a bit alarmed.

> WAI-TUNG
> Pa . . .

Wai-Tung places his finger under Mr. Gao's nostrils. There is breathing. Relieved, Wai-Tung brings back his hand and watches his father sleep. Mr. Gao's is the face of an old man. His skin is dragged and wrinkled, and his mouth can't seem to close, and his eyebrows are locked in a big V. Wai-Tung's eyes begin to moisten. But he fights back the tears and gently nudges his father.

> WAI-TUNG
> Pa . . .

Mr. Gao awakes.

> WAI-TUNG
> Pa, time for breakfast.

> MR. GAO
> Okay, let's go.

Mr. Gao takes the lead. Wai-Tung follows him.

INTERIOR. DINING ROOM. DAY.

The five are eating breakfast.

MR. GAO

Wai-Tung, what are our plans for today?

WAI-TUNG

We'll just stay home this morning. If you want to do some calligraphy, Pa, you can write in my den. Then we'll get married this afternoon.

Mr. and Mrs. Gao both drop their chopsticks and bowls.

MRS. GAO

Get married?

WAI-TUNG

Yeah.

MR. GAO

Who?

WAI-TUNG

Me and Wei-Wei, of course. You wanted to come here to attend our wedding, right?

MRS. GAO

You're getting married this afternoon?

WAI-TUNG

Yeah, why wait? We've already prepared the marriage certificate and we've also reserved a time with the marriage bureau. We scheduled it for two o'clock today.

MRS. GAO

Wai-Tung, we came all this way! How can you be so casual about it?

WAI-TUNG

I told you, Ma, Wei-Wei and I are both very busy and we don't care much for ceremonies. Her parents can't make it so let's keep it simple.

MRS. GAO

This is a milestone in a person's life. You only get married once. You should consider how the bride feels, if not yourself. We collected thirty thousand yuan in gift money in Taiwan. We brought it all here to give you a grand banquet. How can we go back to face our friends and relatives?

WAI-TUNG

I am not getting married to your friends and relatives.

MRS. GAO

If not for friends and relatives then why bother to get married?

WEI-WEI

Ma, it's okay with me. It won't effect our love for each other with or without a wedding banquet. We're not into superficial traditions anyway.

MR. GAO

Very well, they are adults. They have their own plans. We'll just do what they want.

In anger, he rises from the table and goes upstairs.

EXTERIOR. CITY HALL. DAY.

To establish.

INTERIOR. MARRIAGE BUREAU. DAY.

There are a few rows of sparsely populated chairs. A secretary shuffles papers at a desk to the side of the room, while at the front, a nearly comatose bureaucrat presides over the marriage of a pair of grunge rockers.

CLERK

For richer or poorer—

WOMAN

For richer or poorer—

CLERK

In sickness and health—

WOMAN

In sickness and health—

CLERK

Till death do us part.

WOMAN

Till death do us part.

CLERK

Rings. Under the authority vested in me by the State of New York, I now pronounce you husband and wife. You may kiss the bride.

The couple turn to each other and start sloppily making out in front of the assembled onlookers.

The clerk goes to the desk, punches a time clock, and calls out.

> CLERK
> Gao? *(to the kissing rockers)* Uh, excuse me you guys. Thanks.

The newlyweds move on as Wei-Wei and Wai-Tung come forward. Simon takes pictures.

> CLERK
> Umm, no. You need to switch. You're on the other side.

The clerk gestures for Wai-Tung and Wei-Wei to switch. The two oblige.

> CLERK
> Good, now if there is any one here who can show just cause why these two people may not be legally married, speak now, or else hereafter hold your peace. *(pause)* O.K. *(to Wai-Tung)*, now repeat after me. I, Wee-Tong—

> WAI-TUNG
> ''Wai-Tung.''

> CLERK
> Right.

He proceeds to run through the vows with Wai-Tung. Then, he turns to Wei-Wei.

CLERK

I, Wee-wee—

WEI-WEI
(totally nervous)

Wee-wee—

CLERK

Right. Take Wee-Tong to be my lawfully wedded husband—

WEI-WEI

Wee-wee, husband . . . uh, lawful.

CLERK
(pause)

OK. To love and to cherish, to have and to hold, for better or worse, for richer or poorer—

WEI-WEI

Richer is better . . . no, poorer.

CLERK

Uh-huh. In sickness or health, till death do us part.

WEI-WEI

Till sickness and death.

CLERK
(deadpan)

Groovy. Rings. Under the authority vested in me by the state of New York, I now pronounce you husband and wife.

Wai-Tung and Wei-Wei exchange rings, while Simon snaps away from the side.

CLERK

You may kiss your bride.

Wai-Tung quickly and barely pecks Wei-Wei on the cheek.

Mr. and Mrs. Gao look on impassively.

INTERIOR. CITY HALL. DAY.

The group stands in the hallway.

SIMON
(in bad Chinese)

Come on, let's take picture. For posterity!

Simon steps backward and points the camera.

                                SIMON
    Come on, smile! Happy occasion!

*Simon focuses the camera. Suddenly, Mrs. Gao lets out a big cry and begins
sobbing.*

                              WAI-TUNG
    Ma, what's the matter?

Mrs. Gao holds on to Wei-Wei and cries in near hysteria.

                              MRS. GAO
    Wei-Wei, this is all my fault. We came all the way to America for
    nothing. We let you down with such a shabby wedding.

                              WAI-TUNG
    Ma, stop it.

                              WEI-WEI
    Ma, don't say that. I'm very happy.

*Wai-Tung glances at his father, whose face is burning with anger. Simon takes
Wai-Tung aside.*

                                SIMON
    She is so upset, why don't I offer to take everyone out to dinner
    tonight. We'll go to the China Palace. My treat. Let 'em know.

                              WAI-TUNG
    Ma, Simon is taking us to dinner tonight. Let's celebrate. It's the best
    Chinese restaurant in Manhattan.

                               MR. GAO
                          (pointing to Simon)
    We should be treating you!

INTERIOR. CHINESE RESTAURANT. NIGHT.

*A well dressed man in his sixties walks into the restaurant and goes directly to
the counter where the hostess stands.*

                              HOSTESS
    Hi, Boss. How come you're so late?

                                BOSS
                          (in a Hunan accent)
    The traffic on the expressway.

HOSTESS

Oh, really.

BOSS

When did that table come?

The Hostess looks toward where the boss is looking and sees Wai-Tung, Mr. and Mrs. Gao, Wei-Wei and Simon sitting at a large table.

HOSTESS

You mean table C?

BOSS

Right. How long have they been here?

HOSTESS

Oh, for quite a while. They're almost finished.

BOSS

Don't take their money. Go to the kitchen and order two more dishes for them. General Tsao's chicken and pan fried whole fish. I'm going over.

The boss heads to Wai-Tung's table and the hostess heads for the kitchen.

Everyone at the table is eating with their heads bowed. No one says anything. The boss comes up to the table, straightens himself and takes a big bow.

BOSS

Commander!

MR. GAO

It's you, Old Chen!

MRS. GAO

What a coincidence! America is so big and we still run into each other. And in a restaurant no less.

WAI-TUNG

Hi, Old Chen.

OLD CHEN

Madam, young master. I saw you as soon as I walked in.

MR. GAO

You are here to eat?

OLD CHEN

No, . . . I ate at home. Commander, this is my restaurant.

MR. GAO

Your restaurant?

OLD CHEN

Actually, it belongs to my third son, but whatever is his is mine, too.

MR. GAO

Well, congratulations.

MRS. GAO

This is a beautiful restaurant. So, Old Chen, so you finally made it, huh?

OLD CHEN

Madam, if it wasn't for you and the commander, I would be nothing.

MRS. GAO

To think—Old Chang has no restaurant but Old Chen has one. How ironic.

OLD CHEN

I took the liberty of ordering some more food for you. Just two more dishes. It's a small token of appreciation from me. I'll treat the commander, Madam, and Young Master to a big dinner next time.

MRS. GAO

That's not necessary. We are already full. I guess I should call you Boss Chen now, right?

MR. GAO

Why don't you have a seat with us?

OLD CHEN

Commander, Madam, please don't tease me. I do not dare to sit in your presence.

MR. GAO

What kind of talk is this? You're a big boss now. Come on, have a seat.

OLD CHEN

Madam, please just call me Old Chen. And I feel more comfortable standing.

Everyone laughs.

OLD CHEN

Young Master, how long have you been in the U.S.?

WAI-TUNG

About ten years. Stop calling me Young Master. Just call me Wai-Tung, OK?

OLD CHEN

Time really flies, doesn't it? And these two are?

WAI-TUNG

This is Simon, my landlord.

OLD CHEN

I drove the Commanders' jeep for twenty years.

WEI-WEI

Hi, Uncle Chen.

OLD CHEN

And who's this young lady?

MRS. GAO

This is our new daughter-in-law.

OLD CHEN

Young Master, when did you get married? This is not right, I don't have a gift for you. I've got to make up for this.

MRS. GAO

No, you don't have to.

WAI-TUNG

We just got married this afternoon at City Hall. Pa and Ma came here to attend the wedding.

OLD CHEN

Got married at City Hall this afternoon?

WAI-TUNG

That's right. We were having dinner to celebrate and ran into you!

Old Chen bows his head and stares at the half eaten dinner, not saying a word. Mr. and Mrs. Gao are visibly embarrassed.

OLD CHEN

Young master . . . I watched you grow up, so I am entitled to go out of line here to say a few words to you. The Commander is very well known and respected. How can you be so inconsiderate? I am only his servant. But even I, a subordinate, when my third son got married, I had a banquet of twenty round tables—over two hundred people.

Nobody says a word. The waiter brings two more dishes.

WAITER

Boss, pan fried whole fish and General Tsao's chicken.

MRS. GAO

Oh, thank you so much.

OLD CHEN

Our food can not compare to Old Chang's. I hope the Commander won't mind.

MR. GAO

Old Chen, don't be so formal.

Old Chen wants to personally serve the food. He first respectfully places a big piece of fish onto Mr. Gao's plate.

MR. GAO

Thank you.

OLD CHEN

Please allow me, Commander. *(pause)* Hey I've got an idea. Even though you modern kids try to be so hip these days, what is a wedding without a wedding banquet? If you don't mind my place being a little bit small and the food not too great, I would love to have the young master hold his wedding banquet here. What do you think? There is a party room upstairs and above us is a hotel. We can rent a room as the newlyweds' quarter. The bride can change her clothes there too. . . .

WAI-TUNG

That would be too much trouble for you.

OLD CHEN

You think it's trouble, but it's no trouble at all. Old Chen has nothing better to do than to plan a banquet for you. All you have to do is just come to the wedding. Look at that, just the thought of having a banquet brings a smile to the Commander's face.

Mr. Gao won't say yes outright—but he smiles from ear to ear.

OLD CHEN

Young Master. I am not doing this for you. I am doing this for the Commander. The Commander has been to everyone else's banquets for decades. It's time to get back some of those hundred of gifts he gave. If you won't let him have this then you are ungrateful to your parents.

WAI-TUNG

Wouldn't it be too much trouble?

OLD CHEN

Then it's decided. Commander, just leave everything to me. It'll be a great banquet. You will not lose face in America.

SIMON
(to Wai-Tung)

What's up?

Wai-Tung just rolls his eyes.

Dissolve out.

INTERIOR. OFFICE. DAY.

Wai-Tung is going crazy as the phone rings off the hook.

The secretary stands by him with a stack of wedding catalogues to go through.

INTERIOR. SIMON'S BEDROOM. NIGHT.

Simon is awakened by the phone. He picks it up.

SIMON
Hmmm. I knew it was you.

INTERCUT BATHROOM. NIGHT.

WAI-TUNG
(whispering into the cellular phone)
C'mon, I'm in the bathroom. Just like our college days!

SIMON
Uh huh, I'm too tired to get up. And you need all your sleep for the big fucking event.

WAI-TUNG
Yeah. The final act—and then they're out of here.

SIMON
About time. I'm sick of sleeping alone.

WAI-TUNG
I'm sick of the whole thing.

SIMON
You sound tired.

WAI-TUNG
I am. But . . . Let's just talk some more.

SIMON
Okay.

We see the bathroom light spilling into the hallway and hear the muffled tones of their phone call.

EXTERIOR. RIVERSIDE. DAY.

Early morning. Mr. Gao is strolling along the river by himself.

EXTERIOR. WAI-TUNG'S HOME. DAY.

Mr. Gao comes back from his walk. He has his own keys and lets himself into the house.

INTERIOR. WAI-TUNG'S HOME. DAY.

Mrs. Gao is making orange juice. She seems to have familiarized herself with the kitchen now. Mr. Gao enters.

                    MR. GAO
   I didn't walk far today, Only half an hour. I want to save some energy
   for tonight.

Mrs. Gao hands him a glass of fresh juice along with his heart pills. Mr. Gao takes a big gulp then swallows the pills.

                    MR. GAO
   Go wake up Wai-Tung.

Mrs. Gao drops what she's doing and goes upstairs.

INTERIOR. WAI-TUNG'S STUDY. DAY.

Wai-Tung is sleeping on a mattress in his den. Mrs. Gao shakes her head.

                    MRS. GAO
   Wai-Tung, Wai-Tung, time to get up and be the groom! Come on, wake
   up!

                    WAI-TUNG
   Alright.

Just as Wai-Tung gets up, Mr. Gao enters into the den, smiling brightly.

                    MR. GAO
   Morning.

                    WAI-TUNG
   Pa, Ma, go sit on your bed.

INTERIOR. MASTER BEDROOM. DAY.

The three go into the master bedroom. Mr. and Mrs. Gao sit down on the edge of the bed. Wai-Tung kneels down in front of them and takes three full bows. He then gets up an lets his parents each hold him for a little while.

MR. GAO

I wish you a happy life and a long marriage. That's enough.

MRS. GAO

Oh how time flies. It seems like only yesterday when Wai-Tung learned to talk.

MR. GAO

Wai-Tung, do you remember you used to love to sleep on my belly when you were a kid? I'd call out where's Wai-Tung? And you'd say, I am here . . . You were so chubby I wanted to eat you up . . . and you'd just come running. My little fat boy.

WAI-TUNG

I'll go get Wei-Wei ready.

MR. GAO

No. Stay for a while.

MRS. GAO
(grabbing his arm to nibble it)
We probably won't get another chance.

WAI-TUNG

Ma, stop that.

INTERIOR. BEDROOM. MORNING.

Wei-Wei is lying in her bed holding the telephone receiver, waiting. A few seconds later a woman's voice comes over.

MRS. GU

Hello?

WEI-WEI

Ma?

MRS. GU

Wei-Wei, is that you? Why didn't you write us and let us know that you were going to call today? Did you wait long to get a line?

WEI-WEI

Not long. It's alright.

MRS. GU

Why did you call, Wei-Wei?

WEI-WEI

No reason. I just missed you so much. Have you had dinner?

Wai-Tung knocks.

WAI-TUNG

Wei-Wei? Get up and get ready.

Wei-Wei opens the door with phone in hand.

WEI-WEI

I'm already up. Just get ready yourself.

Wei-Wei shuts the door.

INTERIOR. BEAUTY PARLOR. DAY.

With background score, a montage of Wei-Wei getting her hair done and make up applied.

INTERIOR. MASTER BEDROOM. DAY.

Wei-Wei is being fussed over by Mrs. Gao and the tailor's helpers. Mao, already dressed as the bridesmaid, is helping Wei-Wei to put on all her jewelry.

MAO
(in English, so Mrs. Gao won't understand)
They really piled on the rocks.

WEI-WEI

No kidding!

MRS. GAO

Little Sister Mao, thank you so much for your help.

MAO

Don't mention it. It's a pleasure to be Brother Gao's bridesmaid.

Wai-Tung and Simon come into the room as the women gather together, ready to leave.

Wai-Tung looks at his beautiful bride and trades an affectionate glance with her. Simon watches on.

INTERIOR. WAI-TUNG'S HOME. DAY.

The entourage goes downstairs to the living room which is decorated in Chinese red, the color for happiness and extravagance. Mr. Gao, already seated on the couch, is wearing an enormous smile. Mrs. Gao sits next to Mr. Gao as the couple kneels in front of them. The photographer is busy snapping away. Wai-Tung and Wei-Wei bow together three times for the Gaos. The Gaos accept the bows with smiles.

MR. GAO

Alright. Alright. Good.

The Gaos each take out two sets of red envelopes to present to the couple. Wai-Tung and Wei-Wei get up and give the two elders a hug.

MRS. GAO

Sister Mao, please get the lotus soup.

MAO

Thank you, Ma.

WEI-WEI

Thank you, Pa, Ma.

MRS. GAO

We're turning Wai-Tung to you.

MR. GAO

And you, Wai-Tung, must care well for Wei-Wei.

WAI-TUNG

I will.

Mao brings out a big tray from the kitchen. On the tray are four bowls of lotus soup.

MAO

Here, a soup for a quick first son.

WAI-TUNG

Wei-Wei, kneel for the "quick son" soup.

Mrs. Gao takes the soup as Wei-Wei obediently kneels in front of her.

MRS. GAO

Have some lotus soup, a son will come quickly.

WEI-WEI

Come on, Wai-Tung. Kneel down and have some soup with me.

WAI-TUNG
Having a son is a female thing.

MAO
She can't give birth without your help, right?

The entourage laughs as Wai-Tung kneels down and drinks the soup. Wei-Wei dutifully gulps every spoonful that Mrs. Gao feeds her.

MR. GAO
Wai-Tung, Wei-Wei, you two grew up differently. But fate unites the two of you here so far from home. It's something you should treasure. If differences arise . . . opinions . . . habits . . . you must work to resolve them. Always be thoughtful of each other. That's the key to a successful marriage. Seeing you two together today has a special meaning for us. We give thanks to our ancestors. Wei-Wei is a great artist. Wai-Tung, you must help her succeed. Don't let this marriage . . .

Wei-Wei bursts into tears. Mrs. Gao jumps with alarm and drops the soup. She tries to stop the flow of tears by jamming her fingers under Wei-Wei's eyes. It looks as if she might poke them out. She pulls Wei-Wei up by the head and rushes her out of the room.

Wai-Tung wrinkles his nose at this as if this is all some barbaric female ritual.

MRS. GAO
No! No! Don't do that! You'll ruin three hours of make-up! It'll be over soon! Don't cry. Stop talking . . . everything's fine. Stop crying.

The entourage follows the frantic women out the door. Mr. Gao pats Wai-Tung on the back.

MR. GAO
How 'bout that? My speech really touched her, huh?

WAI-TUNG
Yes, pa.

EXTERIOR. NEW YORK STREET. DAY.

A decorated white limousine proceeds through the city.

INTERIOR. CHINATOWN PHOTO STUDIO. DAY.

At the instructions of the studio photographer, Wai-Tung and Wei-Wei stiffly stage different "happy couple" poses. Intercut with the rest of the entourage watching on and encouraging the couple with their own smiles.

STUDIO PHOTOGRAPHER

Would the groom raise his left shoulder. Chin up . . . smile . . . show your white teeth . . . like you love each other . . . turn a little more . . . white teeth . . . smile a little wider. Turn some more . . . okay . . . smile a bit more . . .

The photographer grows impatient as Wei-Wei tries, unsuccessfully, to hold her breath in a perfect pose. The camera clicks.

INTERIOR. HOTEL LOBBY. NIGHT.

The guests file in. Some carry gifts. Some sign the register.

INTERIOR. HOTEL ROOM. NIGHT.

The Gaos, Wei-Wei, Simon, Mao, and a few other friends are standing around in the room making the bed for the newlyweds.

A woman brings a four-year-old boy over to the bed.

OLD WOMAN

Come, "Little Rock" . . . jump on the bed, to make a little boy like you.

The boy happily bounds on the mattress and everyone cheers with delight. The photographer snaps pictures.

INTERIOR. OLD CHEN'S RESTAURANT. NIGHT.

The restaurant has already set up twenty round tables. Most of the guests have arrived and are seated. Wei-Wei and Wai-Tung are paraded past the guests. Simon leads them, Mao holds up Wei-Wei's dress and the Gaos follow behind. The guests rise and applaud the passing entourage.

Mr. Gao and Director Wang exchange courtesies. Then Mr. Gao goes up before the entire room and clears his throat. The crowd quiets down.

MR. GAO

Chief Wang, distinguished guests, my son's marriage to Wei-Wei was very simple, sudden and caught many of you by surprise. With my sincerest apologies, I thank you all for coming.

INTERIOR. RESTAURANT KITCHEN. NIGHT.

The Chef is carving a bird out of a vegetable root.

OLD CHEN

Well, when you gonna finish it?

                              CHEF
Who's talking now?

                              OLD CHEN
The groom's father.

                              CHEF
I got forty minutes.

INTERIOR. RESTAURANT. NIGHT.

The guests are busy feasting away. Noisy conversations mix with the sounds of glasses clicking and bowls and plates rattling.

Someone starts tapping the side of a wine glass. The sound quickly spreads and everyone is clanging their glasses with chopsticks. The din builds.

Wai-Tung whispers to Wei-Wei and the two finally stand up. The crowd quiets down. Wai-Tung gently kisses Wei-Wei on the cheek and then the two of them quickly sit down. The crowd is not satisfied and resumes its clanging even louder.

                              SOMEONE A
That's a kiss? Come on! Put some passion into it!

Wai-Tung and Wei-Wei reluctantly stand up again. Mr. and Mrs. Gao are laughing like everyone else. Simon is expressionless.

Wai-Tung kisses Wei-Wei heavily on the mouth. The crowd roars its approval. Wei-Wei's reaction is contorted. At first, she appears uncomfortable but then she relaxes and enjoys his kiss.

Simon tries to keep his composure. The crowd is happy and the couple returns to their seats. With his napkin, Simon wipes Wei-Wei's lipstick off of Wai-Tung's mouth.

Bob Law stands up.

                              LAW
Quiet everybody!

The crowd quiets down somewhat.

                              LAW
I'm Bob Law. Everyone calls me "The Law." I've known the groom since elementary school. I provided him with his first comic books to amuse himself in class. *(The crowd laughs)* In high school, I took him to the best pool halls. *(The crowd laughs again)* And in college, I got him into parties to score some chicks . . . *(a woman hisses)* er, to meet

some girls. So I was his biggest influence . . . baddest influence, that is. I hope you don't mind Mr. Gao, it's just fun. And after 16 years of friendship, I learned about the wedding only one week before. To everyone who feels as left out as me, I am accepting motions for proper punishment.

Mr. Gao answers with a big laugh.

The crowd agrees and some of them yell, "Fry him!"

Law brings out from behind him a makeshift "chicken", made with just a chicken head, a chicken ass and two wing tips tied to a long string. He dangles the "chicken" in front of Wai-Tung and Wei-Wei, who are staring at him with distrust.

> LAW
> What? You have the guts to get married but not to eat this?

The crowd laughs. Wai-Tung and Wei-Wei each take a reluctant bite. But just as they are about to bite on the chicken, Law pulls the chicken away and the two wind up kissing each other. The crowd is enjoying all this. The two struggle to bite the chicken.

INTERIOR. RESTAURANT. NIGHT.

A Group of Female Guests gather around Wei-Wei. She turns her back to the women and tosses the bouquet behind her. They fight over it and finally Mao comes out holding the bouquet.

A Group of Male Guests gather.

Wei-Wei sits down and Wai-Tung reaches into her dress to remove her garter. She blushes as he turns his back to the crowd and tosses the garter. Bob Law gets it.

> LAW
> This is a cross-cultural event. Everything goes!

Law brings out a handkerchief and blindfolds Wei-Wei with it. He brings her around her table.

A dozen or so male guests rush forward.

The guys take their turn kissing the bride. She is supposed to guess which one is her husband. Wei-Wei shakes her head after each one. Someone brings Wai-Tung over to kiss her and she shakes her head. Then someone else brings over a four year old boy to kiss her. This time Wei-Wei nods her head. The crowd roars with laughter. Wei-Wei takes down her blindfold and seeing the boy, breaks out laughing.

More food is served to the guests. The huge white wedding cake is cut and served as well.

INTERIOR. RESTAURANT. NIGHT.

Wei-Wei is wearing a bright red ChiPao and toasting each table with Wai-Tung. Simon and Mao follow them with bottles in hand. Mr. Gao is toasting another table.

> MRS. GAO

Don't drink so much.

> MR. GAO

I know, I know.

Wai-Tung and Wei-Wei, barely sipping, toast a table of guests about their age.

> GUEST A

Everybody, sit down.

> GUEST B
> *(loudly)*

This is not right. You can't just toast an entire table and just take a short sip. You must toast a full glass to each of us. We all go back a long way.

The Americans, including Steve, Andrew, Haskell, and Marianne, at the previous table watch them with more than a little disdain.

> HASKELL

God, and I thought the Chinese were meek, quiet, math whizzes!

> GUEST C

You're witnessing the results of 5000 years of sexual repression.

> WAI-TUNG

Give me a break! You know I can't drink. I get drunk from beer commercials!

> WEI-WEI

I'll drink for him.

> GUEST D

Protecting him already? Come on, Tofu-head, if you won't drink to us, you must at least drink to Taiwan.

Wei-Wei empties a glass. Wai-Tung empties a glass. So does guest A.

> GUEST D

That's more like it!

GUEST E

Wai-Tung, we haven't seen each other for many years. I drove five hours to be here. Drink with me!

Guest E empties his glass and Wai-Tung does the same. Simon again fills the glasses.

GUEST E

Way to go.

FEMALE GUEST

Wai-Tung, after tonight, all the decent Chinese men in New York are gone. Those left are not worth a burnt egg roll.

GUEST E

Hey, how about me?

FEMALE GUEST

My point exactly! Come on, Wai-Tung, bottoms up.

The female guest and Wai-Tung both empty their glasses. Law runs over to join the fun.

LAW

You guys drinking or talking? My table can't wait any longer. Just cut the crap. We dare you to come over here.

Law waves his arm and the entire banquet hall starts chanting in unison.

ALL

Wai-Tung Gao, we dare you to come over here! Wai-Tung Gao, we dare you to come over here!

GUEST F

Gao? Isn't this the Chen wedding?

GUEST G

The Chen wedding? That's upstairs in the Phoenix Ballroom.

Guests F and G continue eating nonchalantly.

INTERIOR. MEN'S ROOM. NIGHT.

Simon is urinating in the men's room. Three other men are throwing up inside, two into the sink, one into the toilet. The man vomiting in the toilet exits the stall and staggers by Simon. Simon shakes his head, zips up and leaves.

INTERIOR. RESTAURANT. HALLWAY. NIGHT.

Simon walks back into the dining area and sees Law slumped in a chair in the hallway, half dead. Simon heads to the front door where Wei-Wei, holding a platter of sweets, and Wai-Tung are showing the guests the way out. Wai-Tung's face is the color of fresh liver. Wei-Wei is not much better. Mr. and Mrs. Gao are thanking all the guests that are leaving. The restaurant is almost empty. Simon walks up next to Wai-Tung.

SIMON
(to Wei-Wei)

You OK? *(she nods yes)*

Simon looks to Wai-Tung to see if he is alright.

WAI-TUNG
Will you take Ma and Pa home?

SIMON
Yeah, I think I've had enough of this.

MR. AND MRS. GAO
Thank you, thank you for coming. Thank you, thank you very much.

GUEST
Congratulations.

MR. AND MRS. GAO
Get home safe.

GUEST
Congratulations.

SIMON
Mr. and Mrs. Mrs. Gao, me . . . drive . . . home.

MR. GAO
Very well.

WAI-TUNG
Pa, you've really had a little too much tonight, are you alright?

MR. GAO
Just happy.

Mrs. Gao gives Wai-Tung and Wei-Wei each a hug.

MRS. GAO
(to Wei-Wei)

I'll call you tomorrow.

Wai-Tung watches as Simon takes the two elders home. Wai-Tung, feeling very emotional, grabs ahold of Wei-Wei, who naturally leans her head onto Wai-Tung.

Mr. Gao stops to shake Old Chen's hand in the hallway.

MR.GAO

Thank you.

INTERIOR. HOTEL. NIGHT.

Wai-Tung and Wei-Wei take the elevator up to their hotel room. As soon as they get to there, Wai-Tung flops down on the bed, breathing heavily. Wei-Wei, sitting on the edge of the bed, takes off her high heels and rubs her feet. Still drunk, she bursts out laughing.

WAI-TUNG

Are you okay?

WEI-WEI

Ha, ha, ha . . .

Someone knocks.

Wei-Wei stumbles to open the door.

WAI-TUNG

No, don't open the door!

It's too late. A group of friends about Wai-Tung's age storm into the room.

THE GROUP
Surprise! We're invading the newlywed suite.

LAW
You really know how to choose a room, huh? Number 10"69"!

WAI-TUNG

I thought you'd passed out!

LAW
Passed out? Never! And miss the "Newlywed Invasion"? This old glorious tradition we've now brought here!

Egghead brings in a folding table. They set up the table with four chairs.

WEI-WEI

What are you doing?

Egghead covers the table with a white cloth then pours a case of mahjong onto it.

EGGHEAD

My dear Comrade Lovers, we are staying here with you. The long struggle has begun!

Egghead and three others sit down and begin mixing up the mahjong.

WAI-TUNG

Great.

MAO

Wai-Tung, aren't you touched by such friendships?

WAI-TUNG

I am. I am . . .

Guest A brings out a string that's threaded with cherries. Guest B brings out a bottle of liquor and a glass.

GUEST A

Here we go.

GUEST B

Me first, me first.

EXTERIOR. CAR. NIGHT.

Simon is driving. Mr. and Mrs. Gao are seated in the back.

MRS. GAO

Had a little bit too much, huh?

MR. GAO

Yeah . . . but I was so happy.

MRS. GAO

Want your pills?

MR. GAO

Yes . . . I should.

Mrs. Gao takes out a small container from her purse and pours out two tablets for Mr. Gao, who swallows it. From the rear view mirror, Simon can see Mr. Gao smiling contentedly.

INTERIOR. HOTEL. NIGHT.

Wei-Wei is sitting on the bed. Her chest is tied with the string of cherries. Wai-Tung, blindfolded, is trying in vain to eat the cherries off her chest. Wei-Wei laughs. Everyone is having fun. The table is going strong. Mao has joined the game and is with Egghead and two others.

Wai-Tung finally finishes the cherries. Everybody applauds this feat. Wai-Tung takes off his white blindfold and waves it.

GUEST

Another one, another one, last one!

WAI-TUNG

No, I can't take this anymore. Please spare me, guys!

LAW

Okay, he's had enough. We'll leave you alone after one last game.

WAI-TUNG

Another game?

WEI-WEI

Let's do it!

LAW

That's the spirit! Okay, you two get under the covers.

Wai-Tung and Wei-Wei do so.

WAI-TUNG

Oh shit.

LAW

Then take off all your clothes and throw them on the floor. Only when the last piece is off, we'll go.

There is no movement under the cover.

GUEST

Where are the clothes? Are you not man enough?

EGG HEAD

Hey, I'm losing money. I'm not leaving until I win it all back.

LAW

"Every minute in a wedding night is worth a thousand pieces of gold."

There are movements underneath the cover now. Everybody gets excited and encourages them with chants. One piece of clothing after another is flung out from the bed. When the underwear is out, the folks get hysterical.

GUEST C
That's the way! This is great! Beautiful! Just beautiful!

INTERIOR. HOTEL HALLWAY. NIGHT.

The people finally leave, but not without commotion. With the table and the chairs banging around, the group goes into the elevator. The elevator door shuts. Everything is quiet again.

INTERIOR. HOTEL. NIGHT.

Wai-Tung sneaks his head out from underneath the cover to breathe. His face still very red. Wei-Wei pops out too and slides over to Wai-Tung.

WEI-WEI
Will they be back?

WAI-TUNG
I don't think so. I think they had enough fun for one night.

The two close their eyes to rest. The room is filled with heavy breathing. Wai-Tung suddenly opens his eyes.

WAI-TUNG
Wei-Wei, what is your hand doing there?

WEI-WEI
. . . Just . . . resting . . .

WAI-TUNG
Wei-Wei, control yourself . . . Don't do that.

WEI-WEI
Wai-Tung, you are a liar. You said you don't react to women . . .

Wei-Wei jumps on top of Wai-Tung.

WAI-TUNG
What . . . ?

Wei-Wei winces, then her body jerks.

WAI-TUNG
No!

Fade to black.

INTERIOR/EXTERIOR. CAR ON STREET. DAY.

Wai-Tung sits in his car at a traffic light, pensively looking out the window. A car honks behind him, and he realizes he's been blocking traffic. He nervously drives on.

WOMAN IN JEEP

Hey, buddy, watch out!

EXTERIOR. STREET CORNER IN FRONT OF PARKET. DAY.

Simon and two other young activists, one a gay man and the other a woman, are collecting signatures for an Act-Up petition. A middle-aged woman is finishing signing Simon's petition, as Wai-Tung pulls up in the car and honks. Simon smiles, thanks the woman and leaves the petition on the table, saying bye to the others.

EXTERIOR. HOUSE. DAY.

The car pulls up to the house.

INTERIOR. HOUSE. DAY.

Simon and Wai-Tung enter. Simon has his arms wrapped around Wai-Tung who half struggles to walk across the room.

SIMON
(calling upstairs)

Hello?

WAI-TUNG

Hey!

SIMON

C'mon, there's nobody around—and it's been a long time since we did it in the afternoon. C'mon, what's wrong with you?

Wai-Tung smiles, turns around and starts to pull off Simon's shirt. They kiss.

SIMON

Let's go to my room.

Simon runs up the stairs, with Wai-Tung in pursuit.

They run through the upstairs hall, past the open door of the master bedroom—where Mr. Gao sits, fiddling with the blood pressure reader.

Wai-Tung backtracks cautiously to the doorway, not quite believing that he's seen his father. When he does, he straightens up.

                              WAI-TUNG

Ah, Dad. Hi.

Simon joins him at the doorway.

                              MR. GAO

You're back.

                              WAI-TUNG

You didn't go shopping with them?

                              MR. GAO

Shopping is a woman's game. It requires unlimited stamina. I can't keep up with them. I don't feel particularly well today. So I decided to stay home to rest and to write a little. Well, age does take its toll, you know. I only had a couple of drinks and it took me over three weeks to recover. You know what? Simon's gift is really useful.

                              WAI-TUNG

Pa. Don't worry, as soon as your blood pressure lowers a bit you can get on a plane and go home.

Simon comes up to him and fixes it.

                              SIMON

Here. May I?

Mr. Gao doesn't look happy to be helped. Wai-Tung looks away as the sound of the front door opening can be heard.

                              WAI-TUNG

They're back.

He awkwardly exits.

INTERIOR. HOUSE. EVENING.

Mrs. Gao and Wei-Wei come into the house carrying shopping bags of various sizes. Wai-Tung helps them with the bags.

                              WEI-WEI

We can take these. There are more in the car.

Wai-Tung goes outside to get the bags. Mrs. Gao and Wei-Wei drop the bags in the living room.

> MRS. GAO

Oh, I am exhausted.

Wei-Wei goes to the kitchen to get Mrs. Gao a glass of water. Then the two rest on the couch. Wai-Tung comes back in with two big bags.

> WAI-TUNG

Look at all this stuff!

> MRS. GAO

It's a big headache each time I come to America. Wei-Wei went shopping with me for how long? And I still couldn't get enough things. I couldn't afford anything on Fifth Ave. And when we finally found something good and reasonable—it's made in Taiwan.

> WAI-TUNG
> *(to Wei-Wei)*

You tired? Ma is a different person when she enters a department store. She turns into Michael Jordan.

> WEI-WEI

I am not tired. With this much energy, Ma can definitely live 'til one hundred.

Mrs. Gao holds Wei-Wei's arm affectionately and laughs in bliss, but she pauses, noting how tired Wei-Wei really looks.

Mr. Gao comes downstairs with Simon not far behind.

> MR. GAO

Look at the time you get home. They came home before you did and there's no dinner ready.

> MRS. GAO

All you do is complain! These gifts are for your friends. I was just doing your shopping.

> SIMON

I'm ravenous. Let's order in sushi!

Wei-Wei looks disgusted.

> WAI-TUNG

You OK?

> WEI-WEI
> *(weakly)*

Sushi—ick.

INTERIOR. DINING ROOM. EVENING.

The family sits eating the take out sushi, as the doorbell rings.

Simon, who hasn't been eating, runs to get it. It's Marianne.

> SIMON

Hi!

> MARIANNE

You ready?

> SIMON
> *(running upstairs)*

Let me just get my jacket.

> MARIANNE

No rush. We're probably gonna miss the show anyhow. *(noticing the family)* Hey Wai-Tung, Wei-Wei!

> WEI-WEI

Hi.

> MARIANNE

Hope you don't mind us stealing away Simon for the evening.

> WAI-TUNG
> *(obviously jealous)*

Of course not.

> MARIANNE

Haskell's waiting in the car.

> MRS. GAO
> *(in Chinese)*

What's this? Simon going out?

> WEI-WEI

Yes.

> MRS. GAO

Simon has friends? I thought Simon didn't have any friends.

Simon comes downstairs, and heads for the door.

> SIMON

Good night!

MARIANNE

Bye-bye!

WAI-TUNG

Bye, see you. When'll you be back?

But the door closes before there's an answer. Wai-Tung goes back to his food.

INTERIOR. BATHROOM. NIGHT.

Wei-Wei takes a shower, feels odd.

INTERIOR. BEDROOM. NIGHT.

Wei-Wei enters the room as Wai-Tung lies in bed, reading the Wall Street Journal. He barely looks up at her, though she's in a particularly sexy gown. As she lies down, he gets up.

She simply watches him as he cracks the door open onto the empty hallway, looking out for his parents. He shuts the door silently behind him.

INTERIOR. HALLWAY. NIGHT.

Wai-Tung steals down the hallway to Simon's room. He knocks lightly on the door, then opens it. There's no one in the room, and the bed is still made up— Simon hasn't come back from his night out.

Wai-Tung sits on the edge of the bed in the moonlight.

EXTERIOR. NIGHT.

The moon disappears behind some clouds.

INTERIOR. SIMON'S BEDROOM. NIGHT.

Simon quietly enters the room, to find Wai-Tung asleep. Wai-Tung jumps awake, though, as Simon sits next to him.

WAI-TUNG

Where've you been?

SIMON

Out.

WAI-TUNG

What does that mean—out? Out where?

SIMON

Out having a reasonably good time. To the movies. For a drink. I hooked up with Steve and hung out, went to a couple of clubs. You know, like life, remember? Our life?

WAI-TUNG
(almost a whisper)
You having an affair with Steve?

SIMON

Fuck you, okay! Listen, go get a good night's sleep. I just had a really pleasant evening, and I don't feel like dealing with your shit right now. Go.

Wai-Tung gets up and shuffles out, looks back to Simon when he reaches the doorway.

SIMON

Go. Really.

He leaves.

SIMON

Fuck!

INTERIOR. BEDROOM. NIGHT.

Wai-Tung enters the room, and lies quietly down next to Wei-Wei. But soon he realizes that she is crying and turns on the light.

WAI-TUNG
Wei-Wei, Wei-Wei, what's the matter?

WEI-WEI
Don't touch me!

WAI-TUNG
First Simon, now you! Plus my parents are still here. All I do is pamper the four of you—my patience is running thin. Just go to sleep! *(he turns off the light again)* Everything will be fine in the morning.

WEI-WEI
(after a pause)
It feels the worst in the morning!

Another pause.

Suddenly, Wai-Tung leaps up and turns on the light.

WAI-TUNG

What? What are you talking about? What do you mean it—''feels worst in the morning''?

She bursts into tears.

He sinks down onto the bed, holding his head in his hands.

INTERIOR. KITCHEN. MORNING.

Close up of an egg practically incinerated in the pan. Simon comes over and flips it.

SIMON

C'mon, Wei-Wei—I know you can cook an egg. Give it a little thought here.

Wei-Wei throws him a silent look of disgust, then takes the spatula and ruins the eggs.

SIMON
(pissed, leaving)

Just trying to help.

INTERIOR. DINING ROOM. MORNING.

The Gaos and Wei-Wei are sitting at the kitchen table, hearing the muffled sounds of a huge argument taking place outside in the backyard. Suddenly, Simon emerges, furious, followed by Wai-Tung.

WAI-TUNG

But I told you! *(going after him)* Simon!

SIMON

Yeah, you told me you were drunk. You said—and I quote—''things got out of hand.'' Yeah, out of hand and into the—*(noticing the Gaos, who are staring assiduously down at their food)*. Well, what difference does it make, they don't even speak English! You know, Wai, I can say whatever the fuck I want in my own fucking house in my own fucking language.

WEI-WEI

Simon—it wasn't Wai-Tung's fault. I can expl—

SIMON

Oh I don't even care who or what he fucks—but talk about stupid unsafe sex!—*(as Wai-Tung marches out)* Hey! Hey! Hey, I'm talking to you.

Wai-Tung has stormed into the kitchen, and Simon follows for a second.

The parents are still eating, not looking up.

> MRS. GAO
> *(under her breath)*
> Are we overstaying our welcome?

Mr. Gao simply mumbles.

> MR. GAO
> Shut up and eat.

> MRS. GAO
> Did Wai-Tung forget to pay his rent?

From the kitchen their fight can still be heard.

> SIMON
> I mean how much more of this shit do you expect me to put up with?
> Hey—put the fucking phone down and listen to me.

Wai-Tung and Simon re-enter.

> MR. GAO
> *(to Mrs. Gao)*
> You can't put your foot in your mouth if you keep it closed.

> WAI-TUNG
> So where do you get off!? This whole thing was your idea. You fucking
> busybody. Wei-Wei wouldn't even be here but for you, and I wouldn't
> have to deal with any of this shit!

> WEI-WEI
> Shit? I'm shit?! *(crying and leaping from the table)* You're shit—
> you're all shit!

> WAI-TUNG
> I wasn't calling you shit!

> WEI-WEI
> Don't call me anything—you user—you fraud!

She flops down again in her seat.

> WAI-TUNG
> Ah—shit!

He runs out the front door.

The door slams.

The parents look up at Simon, who, flustered, sits down and starts eating. They all eat in silence.

INTERIOR. GYM. DAY.

Wai-Tung listens to incredibly loud rock and roll on his Walkman as he pumps iron like a madman. The camera moves in on his face as the music grows louder and louder.

Fade to black.

INTERIOR. HOUSE. NIGHT.

Wai-Tung enters the empty, dark house. He flips on a light.

He notices the phone message machine flashing, and presses the button.

> SIMON
> *(voice off)*
> Wai-Tung, it's me. Listen, don't be freaked out. Your dad just had a mild stroke—it's not too serious. We're over at St. Sebastian Hospital . . . Um look, about this morning, . . .

Wai-Tung is already out the door before Simon's message is over.

INTERIOR. HOSPITAL WAITING ROOM. NIGHT.

Mrs. Gao is sitting by herself as Wai-Tung bursts in.

> WAI-TUNG
> Ma.

> MRS. GAO
> Oh, Wai-Tung, you're here.

> WAI-TUNG
> How's Pa?

> MRS. GAO
> Sleeping. Visiting hours are over. Don't worry, it's just a mild stroke. The Almighty was looking after him today. But he can't have any more excitement.

> WAI-TUNG
> Oh. Where's Wei-Wei, and Simon?

MRS. GAO

They went to get supper.

Wai-Tung sits down next to Mrs. Gao. She stares at Wai-Tung very strangely with a creepy smile. Wai-Tung is very uncomfortable.

WAI-TUNG

Ma, don't mind about the fight Simon and I had this morning. It's nothing.

MRS. GAO

Wai-Tung . . . Such a big thing. Why did you hide it from us.

Wai-Tung becomes very tense. Slowly he begins to reveal his secret.

WAI-TUNG

I was afraid you couldn't take it. I've been living in a big lie for almost twenty years now. In my life there were many joys and pains I wanted to share with you. But I can't. Sometimes I wanted to just lay it all out to you. But I just couldn't put the burden I've been shouldering for so long onto you.

MRS. GAO

What are you talking about? I was asking you why didn't you tell us Wei-Wei is pregnant. What nonsense are you talking about?

WAI-TUNG
(about to explode)

Ma, I have to tell you something.

MRS. GAO

Actually I've noticed it for a few days now. After you guys fought in the morning, I told her that judging from her bad mood and her complexion she had a boy inside her. As soon as your dad heard that, he fainted.

WAI-TUNG

Ma, quiet down and listen to me.

MRS. GAO

It's good thing Simon was there. Otherwise Wei-Wei and I wouldn't have known what to do.

WAI-TUNG

Ma!

MRS. GAO

Congratulations, Wai-Tung!

She grabs Wai-Tung's arm.

Wai-Tung slings her hand away and lets out a yell.

Mrs. Gao is shocked. Wai-Tung gets up and slams his fist on the wall, and then starts pacing furiously.

WAI-TUNG

Ma, my marriage with Wei-Wei is fake. Simon is my real friend.

MRS. GAO

Friend?

WAI-TUNG

Friend. Lover. Ma, I am gay. Simon is my lover. We've been living together for five years.

A nurse walks through the waiting room.

MRS. GAO
(in total disbelief)
Did Simon lead you astray? How can you be so confused?

WAI-TUNG

Nobody led me astray, Ma. I was born that way.

MRS. GAO

Nonsense! Didn't you have girlfriends in college? Ah—Jean, Lei-Lei . . . you were very intimate with them.

WAI-TUNG

It is because it was the thing to do. Every guy has a girl friend. I couldn't be the exception. Ma . . . it's not easy for homosexuals to find a mate that's so compatible. That's why Simon and I treasure each other. Look at all the so-called normal couples around us. Many of them are feuding if not divorced. They wish they are as loving as Simon and me. So how can you accuse Simon of leading me astray? In fact, if I wasn't so concerned about Pa's desire for a grandchild and your constant matchmaking, I'd have been very content with life the way it was.

MRS. GAO

Is Wei-Wei's child yours?

WAI-TUNG

Yes. The fake marriage was to give her a green card and to satisfy you. But then . . . I don't know . . . we were drunk . . .

MRS. GAO

Don't tell your father this.

WAI-TUNG

I know.

MRS. GAO

It'll kill him.

She begins to cry quietly.

INTERIOR. DOORWAY. SAME TIME.

Wei-Wei stands listening in, with Simon behind her, holding bags of take-out food. She turns to him.

SIMON

He really told her?

She nods yes.

WEI-WEI

Yes, but it's to be a secret from his father.

SIMON

Damn.

INTERIOR. OFFICE. DAY.

Wai-Tung sits alone, thinking. It is deathly quiet.

EXTERIOR. PROMENADE. DAY.

Simon helps Mr. Gao sit. He then gestures to him, helping with some physical therapy exercises. It's obvious Simon has been helping Mr. Gao in this way regularly for some weeks.

SIMON
That's good—not too much. That's alright. Yeah, you got it.

MR. GAO
(muttering, in Chinese)
What a pain in the neck—I wish I had a cigarette!

SIMON
(of course not understanding)
Right, uh-huh, OK, good.

INTERIOR. KITCHEN. DAY.

As Simon cooks, Mrs. Gao quizzes him about his family. Wei-Wei interprets.

MRS. GAO
And where do they live?

WEI-WEI
Where do they live?

SIMON
Well, my mother is in Boston and my father is, I think, in Arizona.

WEI-WEI
Ma in Boston and Pa in Arizona.

MRS. GAO
Ah, how tragic. Where's Arizona?

WEI-WEI
Texas.

MRS. GAO
Does he have any brothers?

WEI-WEI
You have no brothers?

SIMON

Uh, my father, who's quite old now, did have a son by a first marriage, but I never met him—he died in the Vietnam war.

WEI-WEI
(fudging)

No brothers.

MRS. GAO

And two sisters?

WEI-WEI

You have two sisters?

SIMON

Mm-hm. They both live in San Francisco.

WEI-WEI

Yes, they both live in San Francisco.

MRS. GAO

Are they "straight"?

WEI-WEI

Ma!

INTERIOR. DINING ROOM. EVENING.

The family is eating dinner.

MRS. GAO

Simon cooked dinner for us tonight.

MR. GAO

Oh . . . Wei-Wei.

Mr. Gao picks up a piece of meat for Wei-Wei. His arm is still weak from the stroke.

WEI-WEI

Pa, you don't need to serve me meat. There is plenty of meat, you should eat it yourself.

MR. GAO

I have hypertension. I can't eat a fat piece of meat like that. *(to Mrs. Gao)* We should send her something when we get back to Taiwan.

Everyone continues eating.

MR. GAO

I'll do the dishes tonight.

Everyone looks, puzzled, at Mr. Gao.

WAI-TUNG

Why?

MR. GAO

You just eat. After we're done, I'll do the dishes. Simon cooked, I'll wash.

Everyone does what they're told and keeps on eating.

INTERIOR. KITCHEN. NIGHT.

Mr. Gao is trying very hard to wash the dishes. But he can barely control his movements. Everyone else tries to look busy, but is watching nervously. Sure enough, Mr. Gao's hands slip and a plate falls on the floor, shattering pieces everywhere. Wei-Wei quickly gets a broom. Wai-Tung and Simon stoop down to help pick up the pieces.

MRS. GAO

Oh, leave it, leave it.

MR. GAO

I'll pick 'em up. Let me, let me do it.

WEI-WEI

We'll do it. It's nothing. I'll clean it up.

MRS. GAO

Let them do it.

MR. GAO

Then I'll take a bath.

MRS. GAO

I'll go to prepare the tub.

INTERIOR. KITCHEN. LATE NIGHT.

Simon and Wai-Tung are re-doing the dishes. They work calmly, instinctively together. Wai-Tung pauses, looks up at Simon.

WAI-TUNG

Just one more week. And then they're gone.

SIMON

And then what, everything goes back to the way it was? What about Wei-Wei?

WAI-TUNG

First, they go. Then I'll be able to think it through.

SIMON
(pained)

Wai. When they go, I think I might have to go, too.

WAI-TUNG

I know.

They continue with the dishes.

INTERIOR. MASTER BEDROOM. NIGHT.

With a photo album on her lap, Mrs. Gao is sitting on the bed by herself, looking at family photos. Her eyes are red and puffy. Her nose is stuffed. She lifts her head and sees Wei-Wei. She blows her nose with a tissue.

MRS. GAO

Oh, it's you. Wei-Wei, come here.

Wei-Wei enters.

WEI-WEI

Looking at photos, Ma?

MRS. GAO

Sit down with me.

WEI-WEI

This is Wai-Tung as a kid, right? So cute. You looked gorgeous back then, Ma.

Cut to the pictures. Wei-Wei looks at them one by one.

Mrs. Gao blows her nose again. The two share a laugh when they both see a picture of Wai-Tung, a year old, wearing a pair of open-ended shorts (a type of shorts that's popular with rural Chinese, with a hole between the legs for easy peeing), exposing himself.

WEI-WEI

Ma . . .

MRS. GAO

Oh it was tough having Wai-Tung. Not really, we took the risk of getting him out by Cesarean. It almost took my life. And after that the doctor said I couldn't have kids again. Wai-Tung weighed only half the normal weight. I don't know how I raised him. His dad was always away on military duty.

                              WEI-WEI
Ma . . .

                              MRS. GAO
God knows how an infant with a faint heartbeat can become such a big, strong, handsome, normal, healthy and successful young man.

                              WEI-WEI
Ma . . .

                              MRS. GAO
Wai-Tung always did well in school. I didn't spend one second worrying about his grades. I always bragged to my neighbors, this kid cannot be spoiled no matter how I tried.

                              WEI-WEI
Mrs. Gao!

Mrs. Gao is interrupted.

                              WEI-WEI
Mrs. Gao forgive me. I am here to return this.

Wei-Wei gives a shopping bag to Mrs. Gao, who opens it and finds all the gifts she had given to Wei-Wei for the wedding. The red envelopes, the pearl necklace, the bracelets, the ChiPao.

                              MRS. GAO
When a son grows up, mother is nothing anymore.

Mrs. Gao looks at the things inside the bag. Tears stream down her face.

                              WEI-WEI
I am sorry. I didn't know things would turn out like this. I didn't mean to cheat you of your love.

                              MRS. GAO
This, you can return to us. But how about the love we gave to you? How are you going to return it?

                              WEI-WEI
I can't. I can only ask for your forgiveness. But my love for you was real.

Mrs. Gao pushes the gifts back to Wei-Wei.

MRS. GAO

I don't want you to return them.

Wei-Wei pushes them back.

WEI-WEI

I don't want them back. I can't take them.

Mrs. Gao pushes them to Wei-Wei again.

MRS. GAO

I want you to! I want my grandchild!

Wei-Wei pushes the gifts back again.

WEI-WEI

I can't do it. I have my future to think about.

MRS. GAO

Wei-Wei . . . I sometimes envy girls of your generation. You can have an education. You have your own ideas. Your own life. No need to depend on men. You can just do as you please.

WEI-WEI

There is a price to pay for that, too. It's not easy living in America by yourself. That's why I naturally treated you and Pa like my parents. You were my family here.

MRS. GAO

Women are women, after all. Husband and children are still the most important thing to us right?

WEI-WEI

Not really.

MRS. GAO

You're still young. You don't understand yet.

She holds Wei-Wei both for comfort and in desperation.

INTERIOR. WAI-TUNG'S HOME. BEDROOM. NIGHT.

The house is dark. Wei-Wei and Wai-Tung are sleeping on the same bed with their backs to each other. Camera closes in on their faces alternately.

WEI-WEI

Wai-Tung?

WAI-TUNG

Yes?

WEI-WEI

Can you go to the hospital with me tomorrow?

WAI-TUNG

So you've made up your mind?

WEI-WEI

I've already made the appointment for two-thirty. The nurse asked if someone would accompany me. I told her yes.

WAI-TUNG

Hmm.

WEI-WEI

She said it will only take an hour or so.

WAI-TUNG

Hmm.

WEI-WEI

You'll go with me? *(pause)* I sacrificed a little too much for a green card, don't you think?

WAI-TUNG

Don't say that.

WEI-WEI

Maybe there are more important things in this world than to hide in America. We are too selfish. For our own interests, we orchestrated this bogus marriage. We let Simon down. We let your parents down. If we let it continue, we'll let the kid down as well. Starting tomorrow, the lie will be over. I'll go back to China. You'll try to make up with Simon. We can't live this lie anymore.

Wei-Wei can hear Wai-Tung quietly sobbing.

WEI-WEI

Will you go with me?

WAI-TUNG

Promise me one thing. Don't let Pa know.

WEI-WEI

OK. I promise you.

EXTERIOR. WAI-TUNG'S GARDEN. DAY.

Mr. Gao is reading while Mrs. Gao is gardening. Mrs. Gao lifts her head up to look at Mr. Gao, wanting to talk to him.

MRS. GAO
(sighs)

. . . Ah . . .

MR. GAO

What?

MRS. GAO

Nothing.

Mr. Gao goes back to reading while Mrs. Gao hears Wei-Wei and Wai-Tung coming downstairs. She senses something is going on. She puts down her tools and heads inside.

INTERIOR. WAI-TUNG'S LIVING ROOM. DAY.

Wai-Tung and Wei-Wei are heading toward the front door. Mrs. Gao catches up to them.

MRS. GAO

Where are you going?

WEI-WEI

Gonna do a little shopping.

MRS. GAO
I am coming with you.

WAI-TUNG
No, Ma. Stay home and watch over Pa.

MRS. GAO
If I stay home another minute I'll go mad. I am going with you. Wait for me, I'll just get my purse. Don't leave without me! I'm coming right down!

Mrs. Gao hurries upstairs.

INTERIOR. MASTER BEDROOM. DAY.

Mrs. Gao runs into the master bedroom. But her purse is nowhere to be found.

MRS. GAO
Where is it?

Mrs. Gao can't find her purse. She hears the sound of car doors closing and runs over to the window. She sees Wai-Tung starting the car and driving away with Wei-Wei.

She slumps onto the floor, knowing that she has lost her grandchild.

EXTERIOR. GARDEN. DAY.

Mr. Gao rises, and calls to Simon, who he sees inside, gesturing that he'd like a walk. Simon says OK.

EXTERIOR. CAR. DAY.

Camera follows Wai-Tung's car on the street. When they drive past a hamburger place, the camera stops on the shop. The car exits frame, then backs up into the frame and stops in front of the hamburger place.

INTERIOR. CAR. DAY.

WAI-TUNG
You're hungry already? You just had lunch a couple hours ago!

WEI-WEI
I have a sudden craving for a hamburger!

WAI-TUNG
Can this wait? It's almost two.

WEI-WEI

Nope. I must have one now.

EXTERIOR. PROMENADE. DAY.

Mr. Gao motions to Simon that he would like to sit down. They sit. And sit. Then, Mr. Gao pulls out a red envelope, and offers it to Simon. He addresses him in broken English.

MR. GAO

Happy birthday, Simon.

SIMON

Mr. Gao? You speak English?

Mr. Gao just holds up his thumb and forefinger, indicating "just a pinch." He thrusts the envelope into his hand.

MR. GAO

Please. Happy Birthday.

SIMON
(opening the envelope, full of cash, almost laughing)
My birthday! Even I forgot! *(he turns to Mr. Gao)* Then you know, you've known—

MR. GAO

I watch, I hear, I learn. Wai-Tung is my son—so you're my son also.

SIMON
(laughing)
Why you old!—*(now getting serious)* Well, thank you. Thank you. When Wai-Tung—

MR. GAO

No—not Wai-Tung, not mother, not Wei-Wei should know. Our secret.

SIMON

But why?

MR. GAO

For the family.

MR. GAO
(in Chinese)
If I didn't let everyone lie to me, I'd never have gotten my grandchild!

SIMON

I don't understand.

MR. GAO
(smiling)

No—I don't understand.

They continue to sit, watching the boats and the water.

INTERIOR. INSIDE THE PARKED CAR. DAY.

Close up on Wei-Wei. She is only half-way through her burger, chewing every bite deliberately. She has a contemplative expression on her face.

Wai-Tung's getting impatient. He looks at his watch.

WAI-TUNG

It's two-thirty. You can eat while I drive.

Wai-Tung starts the car and is just about to pull out.

WEI-WEI

Don't rush me. You can go by yourself if you want. I'm feeding my baby.

Wai-Tung turns off the engine.

WAI-TUNG

You changed your mind?

WEI-WEI

Yeah.

She takes another bite.

WAI-TUNG

What if you really do want to get married in the future? What will happen to the kid? Have you thought about that?

WEI-WEI

Don't worry, I don't think I could take another wedding banquet. Anyway, it's my own child. I'll find a way.

WAI-TUNG

Having a painting career and a kid at the same time. You think you can handle it?

WEI-WEI

A tough guy has to take responsibility for his actions. If you want to help, you can find me a decent apartment, no rent. Otherwise get the hell out of the way.

Wai-Tung lets out a big smile.

WAI-TUNG

I'm gonna be a father! Maybe I should ask the other tough guy about it.

WEI-WEI

Simon. Yes.

INTERIOR. BACKROOM. DAY.

Simon is on the portable phone.

SIMON

Okay, so they can pick them up at the airport counter, when they check their luggage, right?

A Pause.

SIMON

Two hours before departure, Okay. And that's one low sodium and one healthy heart meal, right? Okay. Thanks.

As he finishes the conversation, Wai-Tung and Wei-Wei enter.

SIMON

How'd it go? You okay?

Wai-Tung and Wei-Wei just look at each other, then tentatively smile at Simon.

WAI-TUNG

Wei-Wei wants to know if you will be one of the fathers of her child.

Simon breaks into a grin, and the other two smile with relief.

SIMON

Sure.

WAI-TUNG

Then—you'll stay?

WEI-WEI

You must, for the sake of the child!

Simon puts his arm around the two of them. Wei-Wei breaks from the circle.

WEI-WEI

Hey, now that I'm keeping the baby, we better go tell Pa he's going to be a grandfather! He'll be so happy!

Simon bursts out laughing.

WAI-TUNG

What's so funny?

SIMON

Uh, nothing—go tell him. I'll be here.

WAI-TUNG

We might as well tell him one true thing—Wei-Wei is having the baby.

SIMON

That's true.

INTERIOR. KITCHEN. DAY.

Wei-Wei prepares tea for Mrs. Gao.

MRS. GAO

Maybe it's just a phase. Perhaps his heart was broken, and he's afraid of women.

WEI-WEI

Ma, it just doesn't work that way.

MRS. GAO

Oh, I know . . . But maybe, when he sees his kid, he'll revert back to normal.

WEI-WEI

I wouldn't bet on it. In the beginning, I was hoping the same thing.

MRS. GAO

I knew it. You weren't totally unhappy in that wedding dress!

EXTERIOR. BACKYARD. DAY.

Mr. Gao dozes as Mrs. Gao sprays weed killer all over the place.

MRS. GAO

This garden will turn back into wilderness when I am gone.

INTERIOR. HALLWAY IN FRONT OF BATHROOM. MORNING.

Wai-Tung sleepily goes to the bathroom door. Just as he opens it, his father emerges, startling him slightly.

MR. GAO
(stiffly)

Good morning, son.

WAI-TUNG

Good morning, Pa.

INTERIOR. AIRPORT LOUNGE. DAY.

The whole gang is there for the departure, sitting and waiting.

Mrs. Gao nudges her husband, who's beginning to doze again.

MRS. GAO

I think it's time.

WAI-TUNG

Ah, yes. And don't forget to bring the wedding pictures with you.

He pulls out a wedding picture album. Mrs. Gao takes the photo book, and opens it. The two elders put on their glasses. They pause over various photos, some funny, some stilted, of the wedding, as Simon and Wai-Tung stand behind to get a better look.

MRS. GAO

This one's great.

More photos, but when Mrs. Gao comes across a photo of Simon with his arms around Wai-Tung, she quickly turns the page, obviously getting upset. Everyone becomes uncomfortable. The first call for boarding is heard.

MR. GAO

Okay, let's go. We really should be going.

INTERIOR. AIRPORT WALKWAY. DAY.

They all gather for a final good-bye.

WEI-WEI
(emotional)

I'll miss you.

MRS. GAO
(to Wei-Wei)

You'll come visit soon.

She hugs Wei-Wei, and then her son, as Mr. Gao addresses Wei-Wei.

MR. GAO

The Gaos will be grateful to you.

Mrs. Gao turns to Simon, who is just about to give her a hug when she freezes up. Mr. Gao takes his hand.

MR. GAO
(to Simon)
Simon. Thank you for taking care of Wai-Tung.

Then the old folks turn and head for the gate.

The three young people are left standing, watching them.

As Mr. and Mrs. Gao walk to the departure gate, Mrs. Gao begins to cry.

Mr. Gao looks at her.

MR. GAO
What's the matter?

MRS. GAO
Nothing. . . . *(lying)* I am just happy.

He takes her arm.

MR. GAO
I am happy too.

As they walk through the security gates, Mr. Gao is briefly frisked by an attendant with a hand-held metal detector.

He lifts his arms, as if in awkward flight.

The End.

KEY PRODUCTION CREDITS

THE WEDDING BANQUET

Directed by:	Ang Lee
Produced by:	Ted Hope, James Schamus, Ang Lee
Written by:	Ang Lee & Neil Peng and
	James Schamus
Associate Producer:	Li-Kong Hsu
Executive Producer:	Jiang Feng-Chyi
Director of Photography:	Jong Lin C.S.C.
Production Designer:	Steve Rosenzweig
Music by:	Mader
Edited by:	Tim Squyres

EAT DRINK MAN WOMAN

Directed by:	Ang Lee
Produced by:	Li-Kong Hsu
Written by:	Hui-Ling Wang & Ang Lee and
	James Schamus
Associate Producer:	Ted Hope and James Schamus
Executive Producer:	Feng-Chyi Jiang
Director of Photography:	Jong Lin C.S.C.
Production Designer:	Fu-Hsuing Lee
Music by:	Mader
Edited by:	Tim Squyres